OZ CLARKE'S
WINE COMPANION

SOUTH OF
FRANCE

SOUTHERN RHÔNE, PROVENCE,
LANGUEDOC-ROUSSILLON

GUIDE
STEPHEN BROOK

De Agostini *Editions*

HOW TO USE THIS BOOK

MAPS
For further information on the wine regions see the Fold-out Map.

Each tour in the book has a map to accompany it. These are not detailed road maps; readers are advised to buy such maps to avoid local navigation difficulties.

▬▬▬ Motorway (*Autoroute*)

▬▬▬ Major road

▭▭▭ Minor road

▭▭▭ Other road

◆ Wine property

FACT FILES
Each tour has an accompanying fact file, which lists sources of information on the region, markets and festivals, and where to buy wine. There is also a short listing of hotels and restaurants.

Ⓗ Hotel
Ⓡ Restaurant

To give an indication of prices, we have used a simple rating system.

Ⓕ Inexpensive
ⒻⒻ Moderate
ⒻⒻⒻ Expensive

WINE PRODUCERS
Producers' names in small capitals refer to entries in the A–Z on page 72.

Visiting arrangements
Ⓥ Visitors welcome
Ⓐ By appointment
Ⓧ No visitors

Wine styles made
Ⓟ Red
Ⓟ White
Ⓟ Rosé
Ⓟ Vin Doux Naturel
Ⓞ Sweet

Please note that guidebook information is inevitably subject to change. We suggest that, wherever possible, you telephone in advance to check addresses, opening times, etc.

While every care has been taken in preparing this guide, the publishers cannot accept any liability for any consequence arising from the use of information contained in it.

First published
by De Agostini Editions
Griffin House
161 Hammersmith Road
London W6 8SD

Distributed in the U.S.
by Stewart, Tabori & Chang,
a division of US Media
Holdings Inc
115 West 18th Street, 5th Floor
New York NY 10011

Distributed in Canada
by General Publishing
Company Ltd
30 Lesmill Road, Don Mills
Ontario M3B 2T6

Oz Clarke's Wine Companion:
South of France
copyright © 1997 Websters
International Publishers

Fold-out Map
copyright © 1997 Websters
International Publishers
Text copyright © 1997
Oz Clarke
Maps copyright © 1997
Websters International Publishers
Some maps and text have been
adapted from *Oz Clarke's Wine
Atlas* copyright © 1995 Websters
International Publishers

Guide
copyright © 1997 Websters
International Publishers

Created and designed by Websters
International Publishers Ltd
Axe & Bottle Court
70 Newcomen Street
London SE1 1YT

UK ISBN: 1 86212 050 1
A CIP catalogue record for this book is available from the British Library.

US ISBN: 1 86212 048 X
Library of Congress Catalog
Card Number 97–66613

OZ CLARKE
Oz Clarke is one of the world's leading wine experts, with a formidable reputation based on his extensive wine knowledge and accessible, no-nonsense approach. He appears regularly on BBC Television and has won all the major wine-writing awards in the USA and UK. His bestselling titles include *Oz Clarke's Wine Atlas*, *Oz Clarke's Pocket Wine Guide* and the *Microsoft Wine Guide* CD-ROM.

STEPHEN BROOK
Stephen Brook is a professional author and journalist, specializing in wine and travel. He writes regularly about wine for *Decanter*, *Wine Spectator* and other periodicals. His books on wine include the award-winning *Liquid Gold: Dessert Wines of the World* and *Sauternes*.

Associate Editorial Director
Fiona Holman
Associate Art Director
Nigel O'Gorman
Art Editor
Christopher Howson
Sub-editor
Gwen Rigby
Editorial Assistant
Emma Richards
Wine Consultant
Phillip Williamson
DTP
Jonathan Harley
Production
Kâren Smith
Index
Naomi Good
Editorial Director
Claire Harcup
Pictorial Cartography
Keith and Sue Gage,
Contour Designs
Pictorial Map Editor
Wink Lorch
Touring Maps
European Map Graphics

Colour separations by Columbia
Offset, Singapore
Printed in Hong Kong

Photographs:
Front cover The Massif de Canigou dominates the landscape west of Perpignan.
Page 1 The Pyrenees are a stunning backdrop to Roussillon's vineyards.
Page 3 Grenache Noir is the predominant red grape variety in the south of France.

Contents

Introduction by Oz Clarke *4*

Wine at a Glance *6*

Regional Food *10*

Touring the South of France *12*

◆

◆

Introduction

High up in the Alpilles the Domaine de Trévallon makes one of the finest red wines in Provence.

This book covers well over one third of all the vineyards in France. Indeed, the Languedoc-Roussillon alone is the biggest vineyard region in the world. Add to this the ancient vines of Provence and the considerable swathes of vines in the southern Rhône and we're talking about a volume of wine produced that is quite daunting.

The hills of Provence were planted with vines by the Greeks as long ago as the 6th century BC, and the Romans had picked out superb sites in the wild mountains of the Languedoc to make wines good enough to be shipped straight back to Rome long before they created France's other great vineyard areas in Bordeaux, the northern Rhône, Burgundy and Champagne. But the French wines that have excelled in the last few hundred years have been those which have actively sought the attentions of connoisseurs in foreign lands, in particular the opinion-formers of northern Europe. With the exception of Châteauneuf-du-Pape, the wines of the southern Rhône and the Medit

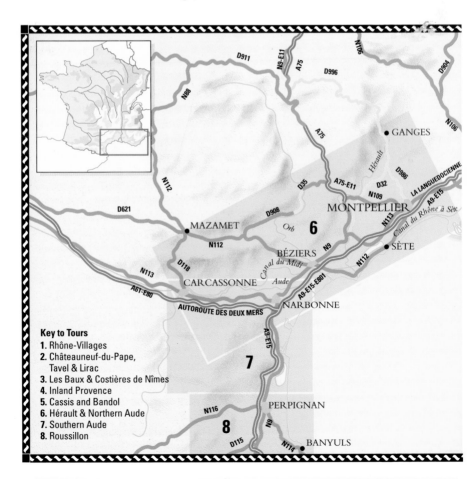

Key to Tours
1. Rhône-Villages
2. Châteauneuf-du-Pape, Tavel & Lirac
3. Les Baux & Costières de Nîmes
4. Inland Provence
5. Cassis and Bandol
6. Hérault & Northern Aude
7. Southern Aude
8. Roussillon

ranean basin harboured humbler ambitions. The Industrial Revolution created a massive, thirsty urban working class in France, and the Languedoc seemed content to supply their needs for cheap wine, while Provence saw little reason to aspire to anything more than satisfying the thirst of glistening, baked holidaymakers sheltering from the midday heat.

The last decade has seen attitudes transformed, as a spirit of innovation has swept through the South. Châteauneuf-du-Pape has regained its position as an internationally respected red wine and Provence has attracted new vineyard owners to its lovely forest glades that tumble down to the sea and to its gaunt, unearthly hinterlands like les Baux-de-Provence. But the biggest thrill is in Languedoc-Roussillon, where a new breed of winemaker – maybe French, maybe English, Belgian, Australian or Dutch – is showing that the New World ideal of affordable, easy-to-understand wines has found a new heartland down by the Mediterranean. While up in the hills, the ancient vineyards are proving that tradition and innovation can make excellent bedfellows.

Oz Clarke

Coteaux du Languedoc red (left) becomes increasingly intensely coloured with age, while Vin de Pays d'Oc Chardonnay (right) deepens to a yellow-gold with short aging.

Wine at a Glance

There's been a revolution in the South of France in recent years. Gone are most of the dull, oxidized and sometimes really nasty wines. Investment, wine-making expertise and innovation have resulted in a whole range of fresh, fruity and vibrant reds, whites and rosés, and excellent sparklers, fortified reds and sweet wines, and there are outstanding prices to match the exciting flavours.

Grape Varieties

Many of the best wines are being made from good-quality traditional grapes as well as the newly arrived international varieties, but innovative blends of both have also emerged. Organic and biodynamic cultivation of the vine are practised more widely here than anywhere else in France.

Grenache Noir

The second most widely planted grape in the world likes hot, dry climates and is grown extensively in southern France. It reaches its peak in the southern Rhône, especially in Châteauneuf-du-Pape, where it is the most important of the 13 varieties allowed in the blend. Here it combines great alcoholic strength with

Grenache Noir

rich raspberry fruit and a perfume hot from the herb-strewn hills. It is generally given more tannin and acid by blending with Syrah, Cinsaut or other southern French grapes. It can make wonderful rosé in Lirac, Tavel and Côtes de Provence. In Rasteau, in the southern Rhône and in Banyuls and Maury in Languedoc-Roussillon, it also makes thick, sweet fortified reds.

Mourvèdre

This variety needs lots of sunshine to ripen and therefore does well on the Mediterranean coast at Bandol, where it plays a starring role, producing wines with a good tannic

Mourvèdre

backbone that can age for 20 years or more. Much overlooked elsewhere in the region until recently, its importance as a source of colour, body and pine-needle aroma has led to increased plantings during the past couple of decades.

Syrah

Only in the last 30 years has this great red grape extended south through the southern Rhône and the Midi from its heartland in Côte-Rôtie and Hermitage in the northern Rhône. Though much valued as an 'improving' variety for Grenache,

Syrah

an increasing number of varietal wines are emerging from cooler sites in the Languedoc. From low yields in warm, rather than hot, conditions the wine has a more perfumed and classic peppery character.

Chardonnay

Chardonnay adapts well to southern France's hot climate. A wave of new varietal Vins de Pays is emerging, particularly from the Ardèche and Languedoc. Some of these early wines were alcoholic, quickly becoming flabby, but now some riper melony flavours have been captured in a slightly leaner style that ages well for a few years.

Chardonnay

Viognier

This fashionable white grape is sprouting all over southern France. Modelled on the expensive Condrieu of the northern Rhône, Viognier is not proving easy to shape into the exotic, voluptuous seducer sometimes seen there. Much is made of its low yields, but it needs skilled wine-making in order to produce balanced examples. Even if lighter and more delicate than the best Condrieu, southern French Viognier can combine an inviting perfume with a rich peachy, apricot fruit, and with more vine age should show increasing depth and concentration.

Viognier

Other Varieties

Carignan is southern France's main red grape and is mostly blended with Grenache Noir and Cinsaut. When made from low-yielding old vines, the wine can show real quality, even as a varietal. Cabernet Sauvignon is the most popular of the new reds, and has also been blended successfully with Syrah in Provence and in Languedoc's most famous red from Mas de Daumas Gassac. Grenache Blanc is important in complementing Clairette and Bourboulenc, a traditional blend for southern French white. Muscat is used for fortified whites in Beaumes-de-Venise and in Languedoc-Roussillon, especially at Rivesaltes and Frontignan.

CLASSIFICATIONS
Regional AC The most basic appellation with specific criteria but no further geographical definition, e.g. Côtes du Rhône.
Regional AC with a geographical definition Requires lower maximum yields and a higher minimum alcohol level. If from a single village, the name may be added, e.g. Côtes du Rhône-Villages – Cairanne.
Village AC E.g. Vacqueyras – a former Côtes du Rhône-Villages but promoted to its own AC. There is no further vineyard or site classification.
Vin Délimité de Qualité Supérieure (VDQS) A kind of junior AC.
Vin de Pays There are three levels: regional, departmental and zonal. Vin de Pays d'Oc sweeps up a lot of wines and many of the dozens of individual zonal names are rarely used.
Vin de Table Accounts for over 20 per cent of the harvest. Much is sold in bulk or distilled.

Understanding Southern French Wine

You can learn something about a wine simply by looking at the bottle. Here, traditional shapes rub shoulders with innovative modern packaging.

The level of fill usually comes to just below the bottom of the cork, but the gap – or ullage – slowly increases with age, though it should remain small. Only wines that have been kept for 10 years or more will have a significant ullage.

The classic Burgundy-shaped bottle is used for Châteauneuf-du-Pape but only estate-bottled wines can have the name of the appellation and old papal coat of arms embossed on the glass.

This wine estate uses biodynamic methods of viticulture and vinification.

The wine laws devised for Châteauneuf-du-Pape in 1923 formed the basis for France's entire AC system, first created in 1935.

DOMAINE DE MARCOUX
1993
CHATEAUNEUF du PAPE

EU regulations now require the capsule to be made from tin foil or plastic instead of lead.

Coloured glass helps protect wine from the harmful effect of light. Here, a very pale olive-green glass has been used to enhance the colour of the wine.

The embossed glass and small, classy-looking label are part of a radical modern look for the wines of Languedoc-Roussillon, projecting this wine as one in a range of quality varietals.

Fortant de France is the trade name of Robert Skalli, a leading innovative producer in southern France. This wine is part of the top-of-the line 'Collection' range.

The typography on the label emphasizes the grape variety, Viognier, and the producer's name rather than the wine's classification, Vin de Pays d'Oc.

VIN DE PAYS VERSUS AC

The classification of quality French wine has always been based on delimiting geographically precise vineyard areas. The Vin de Pays category, with loose geographical strictures but quite strict production regulations, was finally formalized in 1979, mainly to help the Midi, which had been a virtual monoculture of the vine, but based on quantity not quality. During the 1980s the EU provided incentives to encourage the production of quality wines, and this resulted in considerable investment in the region's vineyards, and in radical wine-making practices that included the increased use of the so-called 'international' grape varieties.

The AC laws, based on making a wine 'typical of its place', allow a range of different 'native' or traditional grape varieties but the use of others previously unknown in the region is banned. Innovative producers could, therefore, label their wines only as simple Vins de Pays.

The opportunity to name and emphasize a grape variety on the label puts these hitherto unknown southern French wines on the same marketing plane as their highly successful New World competitors. And it is this that provides the real spur to makers of innovative, quality wines.

How to Choose Southern French Wine

The South of France is currently at the centre of a debate concerning the classification, labelling and marketing of its newer wines. Many of these are varietal wines, named after the grape variety (or varieties) used, rather than the more traditional blended wines. The region produces myriad wine styles, both traditional and new, and the label reveals much about the style and quality of the wine inside the bottle. All French wine labels are required to state certain basic information, but many producers of new southern French wines, especially branded wines, follow their New World counterparts and use innovatively designed, eye-catching labels as an important marketing tool.

A small but highly regarded AC in the coastal hills between Marseille and Toulon.

The producer, Château de Pibarnon, is a small, well-sited estate making red, white and rosé wines.

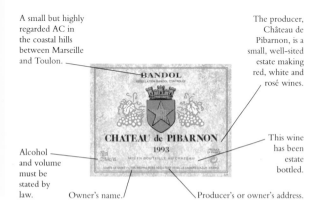

Alcohol and volume must be stated by law.

Owner's name.

This wine has been estate bottled.

Producer's or owner's address.

Understanding Vin Doux Naturel

Vin Doux Naturel (or VDN) is the principal fortified wine style in the South of France. The whites are made from the Muscat grape and the reds from Grenache Noir. These grapes achieve very high natural sugar levels in the hot Mediterranean sun. The wines are made by a process called *mutage*, whereby fermentation is halted soon after it has begun by the addition of grape spirit (95 per cent proof), giving wines that are deliciously unctuous.

Languedoc-Roussillon produces several fortified Muscats (Frontignan is the most famous and Rivesaltes the most up-to-date and attractive), but the best known outside France is Muscat de Beaumes-de-Venise from the southern Rhône. Despite its high alcohol level (16 per cent is typical), it is one of the lightest sweet wines made, only half-sweet but full of delicious grapy flavours. Unlike most other sweet wines, it is relatively inexpensive to make, thanks to its fairly simple method of production. Vintage is not of any real importance, but the wine should be drunk when it is still young, either chilled as an apéritif or as a light dessert wine.

The best fortified red is Roussillon's Banyuls – France's answer to Port, being produced in a fundamentally similar way. Some Banyuls capture the essence of the grape, others are aged in wood or given a more oxidative aging, often in warm conditions to produce a *rancio* version. Rich and sweet, its flavours include dark cherry and plum, dried raisins and prunes, nuts (especially walnuts) and licorice.

VINTAGES
Most southern French white and rosé wines should be drunk as young as possible. The reds vary in style, so merit less generalized assessment.
Southern Rhône
Only Châteauneuf-du-Pape and a handful of exceptional wines from Gigondas, Vacqueyras and Côtes du Rhône have the potential to age for a decade or more. Vintages for Châteauneuf-du-Pape apply only to the more concentrated versions – the lighter, fruitier versions should be drunk within 3–4 years. This AC has also witnessed an explosion of *cuvées spéciales*, so there are now wines of greater aging potential. Concentrated whites for aging, such as Châteauneuf-du-Pape, are far less common. (See also below.)
Provence
Bandol can age for at least 10 years, as can the best reds from elsewhere in the region, such as Domaine de Trévallon.
Languedoc-Roussillon
Exceptional reds from Mas de Daumas Gassac can last for a decade. Red Vin Doux Naturel, Banyuls and Maury from an older vintage can be good too. The best Fitou, St-Chinian, Collioure, Coteaux du Languedoc reds and Vins de Pays can improve with 3–5 years' aging.
Recent Vintages (Châteauneuf-du-Pape)
1996 A rainy year and variable quality, so stick to top names.
1995 Some very exciting and ageworthy wines.
1994 Rain at vintage time did not spoil this good, often very good, year, with soft wines ready for drinking soon.
1993 Although affected by rain, the wines are good to very good, if lacking in consistency.
1992 Variable quality but there are some individual successes.
1991 Not as good as previous years, but some reasonable individual wines.
1990 The last of a trio of truly outstanding vintages. Some very good wines already, but many could improve even further with another 10 years' aging.
1989 Wonderful wines that may improve for another 10 years.
1988 The firmer style was initially a little unrewarding, but some are now developing well.
Older Vintages 1986 produced a few good wines, although they are otherwise variable. The best 85s can still improve, but most should be enjoyed now, and also any 83s. The best wines from the excellent 81 vintage are still likely to be superb.
Other good years 1979 78 70 67 61.

The capsule bears the name and crest of the producer for easy identification in a rack.

Clear glass is traditionally used for sweet white wines in order to highlight the delicate golden colour of the wine.

This producer makes outstanding VDN, as well as a range of Roussillon red and white table wines.

The wine should be drunk within two or three years of the vintage. Aging will be more rapid in this half-bottle size.

Muscat de Rivesaltes is by far the biggest Muscat appellation in France.

This small punt has no significant purpose.

This is a half-bottle (37.5cl), but a full bottle (75cl) is more common for the Languedoc's fortified Muscats.

Bouillabaisse, *a thick stew of Mediterranean fish, is the most famous Provençal dish.*

Regional Food

Southern France is given its gastronomic personality by the Mediterranean. The mild winters and hot summers allow the olive to flourish here, and this defines the cooking of the region. The excellence of local olive oils diminishes the need for butter and cream in cooking. The abundance of fish, vegetables and fruits gives a freshness and lightness to southern French cooking, with far less reliance on tarts, eggs, potatoes and rich meats. Inland, where game is prized, the cooking is more substantial, but it is always tempered by the omnipresence of garlic and fresh herbs.

Regional Produce

Provence, with its abundance of olives, fish, herbs and garlic, has established the character of southern French cooking. However, this style of cuisine is encountered right across the region, with significant regional variations in areas such as Roussillon, with its powerful Catalan influences.

But there is great variety within the region. Along the coast there is an abundance of fish. In the mountains you'll find a profusion of stews and dried and cured meats. Game is plentiful in the hills of the Languedoc, and dishes such as hare, thrush and wild boar feature on many menus. In the Minervois there are influences from the Toulouse district, and you find dishes such as *cassoulet* or *confit*. Moreover, there are, inevitably, influences from outside the region. Along the Côte d'Azur, there are strong Italian accents. In Toulon and Marseille you will find a large number of North-African restaurants offering *couscous* and other classic dishes from Algeria and Morocco.

Because Mediterranean fish tend to be spiny and bony, many are stewed or made into soups. Fish cooked and served whole – such as *dorade* (John Dory), *loup* (sea bass), *rouget* (red mullet) and *rascasse* (scorpion fish) – are becoming increasingly rare and expensive. In the Camargue you may encounter *bouriroun* (elvers, usually cooked with eggs).

The best meat is usually lamb, reared around Sisteron in Provence or on the Cerdagne plateau in Roussillon. It is commonly sprinkled with rosemary and other herbs and roasted. Rabbit is often cooked with mustard or stewed with tomatoes and garlic. Southern France is no place for steaks, and beef tends to be stewed as a *daube* with tomatoes, peppers, onions and garlic; beef is, however, a speciality of the Camargue. In Roussillon you can sometimes find bull, usually just after a bullfight! Game birds are common in the Languedoc hills, notably *perdrix* (partridge) or *grive* (thrush).

Vegetables are abundant and there are delicious seasonal specialities, such as wild asparagus, baby artichokes or the

---

MATCHING WINE AND FOOD

Like the wines of southern France, the principal dishes are strongly flavoured, so there is no difficulty in matching food with appropriate wines.

Fish soups and stews are often highly flavoured and need a fairly robust wine. With *bourride* or *soupe de poissons* try a Mourvèdre rosé, either from Bandol or a good *vin de pays*. Cassis, white Bandol and white Châteauneuf-du-Pape go well with fish – *rascasse, rouget* or *dorade*. In Languedoc Picpoul de Pinet is the perfect wine to drink with the abundant oysters and shellfish found on the coast near Montpellier.

Lamb scented with herbs is the most popular meat dish in the south, especially in Provence. A wide range of wines will go well with lamb dishes: try Coteaux d'Aix, Pic St-Loup or Côtes du Roussillon-Villages. In the autumn and winter, game dishes abound and these need a more robust wine. Good choices include Châteauneuf-du-Pape, Lirac or a mature Bandol; or the slightly less alchoholic Faugères or St-Chinian.

Since most cheeses are made from sheep's milk, red wine is not an ideal accompaniment. Try a fresh dry white, such as Chardonnay from La Clape.

As for Vins Doux Naturels, Muscat is usually served as an aperitif, but a Grenache-based VDN is perfect with fruit-based desserts. Anything made with figs, peaches or nuts will go beautifully with an aged Rivesaltes or Banyuls, whereas chocolate-based desserts work surprisingly well with vintage-style VDNs such as Maury or Banyuls Rimage.

tiny wild leeks of Corbières. In autumn, wild mushrooms begin to appear on the menus of top restaurants. Black truffles are found around Mont Ventoux as well as near Valréas, Carpentras and in parts of the Languedoc such as Corbières.

Cheeses are not especially exciting and cannot compete in terms of variety with Normandy or Burgundy. Many are made from goat's milk, and Provence does produce one superlative cheese, Banon, a roundel of goat's cheese wrapped in chestnut leaves and rinsed with the grape spirit *marc*. In Roussillon you will come across excellent *brébis* cheese, made from ewe's milk.

Fruit is abundant in summer: melons from Cavaillon stacked by the roadside, succulent peaches, figs from around Marseille, grapes from Carpentras. Given the quality of local fruit, it is not surprising that there are few desserts of any note. However, there are local specialities worth looking out for and excellent honeys are found everywhere – lavender honey can be particularly good.

The best place to buy fresh food is at the markets. Most villages have weekly ones, some of which are very good, and towns such as Béziers or Narbonne have excellent daily covered markets called Les Halles. Fish can be bought at the quayside in ports such as Marseille, and lovers of oysters and other shellfish can gorge themselves in the restaurants and snack bars of Bouzigues and Mèze south-west of Montpellier.

Eating Out

Although there are some luxurious restaurants along the coast and in large towns, most of those you encounter will be small and unpretentious. Nevertheless, they often serve delicious food, based on local traditions.

Lovers of *haute cuisine* will find many great chefs in the South: Clément Bruno in Lorgues (see Chez Bruno p.38), the Pourcel brothers in Montpellier (see Le Jardin des Sens p.53), David Moreno in Durban-Corbières (see Le Moulin p.62), Gilles Goujon in Fontjoncousse (see Auberge du Vieux Puits p.62) and Didier Banyols in Céret (see Les Feuillants p.68). Should you wish to eat at one of these top restaurants, an experience no food lover should miss, remember that set meals are almost always cheaper at lunchtime and you are less likely to need to reserve a table.

Much is written about the mysteries of eating out in France, but there are few countries in which the process is simpler. Menus are always displayed outside the restaurant, so you can study them at leisure before entering. Tax and service are invariably included, so if a menu is priced at 200F, that is the sum you should be charged, plus drinks. However, mark-ups on wine are very high and can double the cost of the meal. Don't hesitate to ask the *sommelier* for a single glass, if that is what you require.

REGIONAL SPECIALITIES

Tapenade Intensely flavoured paste made from black olives, anchovies, olive oil, lemon juice and capers. Eaten with bread.
Anchois Anchovies; served with fresh red peppers these are a speciality of Collioure.
Pistou Sauce based on basil, garlic and pine nuts; served with vegetable soups.
Aïoli Garlicky mayonnaise with lemon juice, served with fish, potatoes and fish soup.
Rouille Mayonnaise of olive oil, garlic, chilli pepper, bread and fish broth, served with fish soups.
Soupe de poisson Spicy, clear fish soup, served with croutons, grated cheese, olive oil, garlic and sweet peppers.
Bourride Soup made with white fish, onions and tomatoes and thickened with eggs and aïoli.
Bouillabaisse A soup so stuffed with fish that it is a meal in itself. The broth is seasoned with *rouille* and poured over garlic croutons.
Loup aux fenouille Sea bass grilled over fennel twigs.
Brandade de morue A creamy dish made from salt cod, olive oil, herbs and milk.
Petit-gris Small land-snails from Corbières.
Estouffade de boeuf Beef stewed with onions, garlic, wine and olives and flavoured with orange. A speciality of the Camargue.,
Carn de parol Pressed pork slices, incorporating bits of ear and cheek, from Roussillon.
Pieds et paquets Marseillais dish of sheep's tripe stuffed with onions, garlic, tomatoes and salt pork and sometimes served with sheep's trotters.
Cassoulet Hearty dish of beans, sausages and preserved meats.
Confit Pieces of duck or goose preserved in their own fat.
Petites pâtes à Pézenas Pastry ovals filled with curried minced mutton, brown sugar and lemon zest – introduced to the town by the Indian cooks of Clive of India when he stayed there in 1768.
Aligot Mashed potatoes with butter or cream and cheese, flavoured with garlic.
Ratatouille Tomatoes, onions, aubergines, courgettes and peppers stewed with olive oil and garlic.
Calissons Oval-shaped marzipan biscuits from Aix.
Navettes Boat-shaped biscuits from Marseille.
Papalines Orange-flavoured chocolates from Avignon.
Marrons glacés Candied chestnuts from Collobrières.
Candied and crystallized fruits A speciality of St-Rémy.

Lavender fields intermingle with vineyards near the village of St-Pantaléon-les-Vignes in the Drôme.

SUMMARY OF TOURS

Rhône-Villages Compact and easy-to-visit region of medieval villages with rich red wines.

Châteauneuf-du-Pape, Tavel and Lirac A visit to the plateau where one of France's most powerful reds and also aromatic whites flourish, and a look at the only rosé AC in the region.

Les Baux-de-Provence and Costières de Nîmes Set in the heart of a wild landscape, the fascinating village of les Baux is also a gastronomic paradise. The Costières is a source of delicious, inexpensive wines.

Inland Provence This vast region encompasses some excellent wine estates between St-Tropez and Salon and is a wonderful way of combining wine-tasting with visits to lovely towns such as Aix-en-Provence.

Cassis and Bandol A visit to Cassis gives you a glimpse of the glamorous coastal resort, as well as a chance to taste some fine white wines. At Bandol you can gamble in the casino and try some powerfully flavoured reds and fashionable rosés.

Hérault and Northern Aude This region, once despised by wine lovers, is now a source of delicious and varied wines at bargain prices.

Southern Aude The Corbières region offers beautiful mountain scenery, as well as superb restaurants.

Roussillon This is Catalan country, rich in local traditions and famous for its succulent and long-lived fortified wines.

Touring the South of France

Visiting the wine regions of the South of France is an excellent way to tour a fascinating area. Most of the regions are rural, but the influx of new residents to the South in search of winter sunshine means that vineyard owners in Cassis and Bandol must compete with property developers.

These tours begin in the eastern part of Provence. There are a few vineyards behind the Côte d'Azur, but they are insignificant. From St-Tropez, however, the vineyards stretch westward almost continuously up to the Spanish border beyond Banyuls, and some appellations such as Côtes de Provence or Coteaux du Languedoc are widely dispersed. This makes visiting the wine regions quite time-consuming. Only a few areas, such as Châteauneuf-du-Pape, Bandol and Faugères, are relatively compact. Fortunately, roads are excellent, and in some places, such as around Aix, Avignon and Perpignan, *autoroutes* will speed you through the more built-up areas. In mountainous areas such as Corbières, travelling can be slow; but although the roads are narrow and winding, they are well maintained.

Accommodation can be a problem away from the main towns. Some rural areas such as the Côtes de Provence and Corbières are not well served with hotels, and those that do exist are often of a minimal standard. It is often better to stay in a city or market town, where one can also take advantage of a wider range of restaurants. Many country hotels are small, so if you are travelling in summer it is wise to book ahead. You can find *chambres d'hôtes* – bed and breakfast – in many rural areas, a type of accommodation you either adore because it brings you into personal contact with local people, or detest for the relative lack of privacy.

The best seasons in which to visit the vineyards are spring or late autumn, when there are fewer crowds. Summer can be very hot and far from ideal for touring; some areas are fairly arid and short on shade, so picnicking can be difficult. Avoid September and early October, when estates are harvesting and have no time for visitors.

Wine festivals, held at various times of the year, are more common in Provence than in Languedoc-Roussillon. Some are modest affairs in a village square, others, such as the Avignon fair, more organized. They can be enjoyable occasions on which to meet local producers, but often the top estates don't participate. Since most estates are equipped to receive visitors and allow them to taste their current wines, that is often the better way to become acquainted with the region's best wines.

Rhône-Villages

The Côtes du Rhône-Villages is a large sprawling region dispersed between three departments, the Vaucluse, the Gard and the Drôme. The only nearby town of any size is Orange. Once a mighty Roman city, it is today somewhat scruffy, quite overwhelmed by its magnificent antique remains: the three-bayed triumphal arch, now consigned to a traffic island, and the remarkably well-preserved theatre.

The Tour

Although this tour includes many of the best estates of the southern Rhône, it is a large region so don't be afraid to leave the beaten track and visit little-known domaines and wine villages. Almost all the wine estates and co-operatives have tasting rooms and can usually be visited without an appointment. Some of the more obscure villages include Visan and Valréas in the north.

Like many wine villages in the southern Rhône, Cairanne has wonderful views of the surrounding vineyards from its hilltop setting.

Leave Orange by heading north-east on the N7, then take the D976 to the sleepy but pretty villages of Sérignan-du-Comtat and Ste-Cécile-les-Vignes. From Ste-Cécile turn right on the D8 to Cairanne, which produces many outstanding wines and has the highest concentration of top-class estates of any of the Villages. The route gives you a first glimpse of the jagged edges of the small but dramatic mountain range called the Dentelles de Montmirail, with the shapely bulk of Mont Ventoux looming behind.

Cairanne is a pretty hilltop village with many of its medieval ramparts still in place. Along the turning to the left, leading to the old village, is the Domaine de l'Oratoire St-Martin, perhaps the best estate in the village, where the energetic Marcel Richaud makes a range of sound wines, including Cuvée l'Ebrascade from very old vines. Other domaines are accessible from the D69 road to Rasteau. Domaine Rabasse-Charavin is also worth a visit, and there is a large range of wines to taste and buy here and at the Cave de Cairanne, the reliable co-operative in the village itself.

Continue toward Rasteau and turn right at its local co-operative, the Cave des Vignerons. Soon you will reach Domaine de la Soumade, where André Roméro makes some astonishingly dense and concentrated wines and a delicious fortified red. The vineyards here are gently sloping and the best of them give red wines that can rival Vacqueyras and Gigondas for power and richness. A speciality of Rasteau is a sweet wine made from fortified Grenache.

From la Soumade turn back and head for Roaix and thence north along the winding D20; when it joins the D94, turn right in the direction of Nyons. You are no longer in the Vaucluse department, but in the Drôme. This

TOUR SUMMARY

This long tour starts and finishes in Orange. It takes in some of the best Côtes du Rhône-Villages wine estates in the foothills of the Dentelles de Montmirail and also visits the AC villages of Gigondas and Vacqueyras, and Beaumes-de-Venise, famous for its Muscat wine. There is an optional trip to the bustling town of Carpentras and the beautiful Mont Ventoux region.

Distance covered 150km (90 miles).

Time needed 2 days.

Terrain Despite the distances, it is not a difficult region to tour, and the roads are fast and rarely crowded. The flat land around the Rhône gradually gives way in the east to the hills of the Dentelles de Montmirail.

Hotels Recently, a few good country hotels have sprung up – sometimes on the wine estates themselves – but, in general, towns such as Orange and Vaison make better bases.

Restaurants The towns offer a wide selection of restaurants and there are places serving good food in one or two of the villages and on the wine estates.

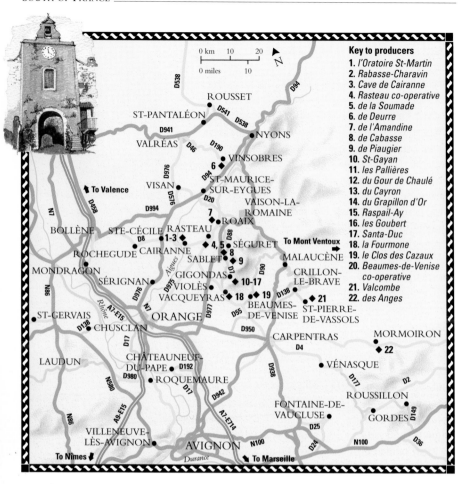

Key to producers
1. l'Oratoire St-Martin
2. Rabasse-Charavin
3. Cave de Cairanne
4. Rasteau co-operative
5. de la Soumade
6. de Deurre
7. de l'Amandine
8. de Cabasse
9. de Piaugier
10. St-Gayan
11. les Pallières
12. du Gour de Chaulé
13. du Cayron
14. du Grapillon d'Or
15. Raspail-Ay
16. les Goubert
17. Santa-Duc
18. la Fourmone
19. le Clos des Cazaux
20. Beaumes-de-Venise co-operative
21. Valcombe
22. des Anges

Map illustration: the medieval gateway at Rasteau.

is still the Côtes du Rhône-Villages region, but the more northerly location gives the wines a character that is generally less burly and powerful than those from the Vaucluse. Just before Vinsobres, stop at the Domaine de Deurre, where Hubert Valayer will pour you good wines from two Drôme villages, St-Maurice and Vinsobres.

You are now close to Vaison-la-Romaine, an excellent base with a fair selection of hotels and restaurants. As well as the charming medieval *ville haute* perched on a cliff beneath the ruins of a medieval château, there are extensive Roman remains near the main part of the town.

From Vaison take the D88 to Séguret, a village known for its robust red wines. Turn right toward Roaix, and on the right is the Domaine de l'Amandine, which produces rich, satisfying Séguret wine in a warming, old-fashioned style. The owner's British son-in-law can assist if you have language difficulties. Return to the D88 and drive up to the medieval hilltop village of Séguret, the most charming along the slopes of the Dentelles. La Table du Comtat is probably the best restaurant in this region and is an ideal spot for dinner and an overnight stay.

Descend toward Sablet and on the right is the Domaine de Cabasse, snuggled into a hollow. Here, in one spot, you'll find a hotel, restaurant and wine estate. Although perfectly located as a base for wine tourism, the temptation to spend all day by the pool may be too great for some. The Haenis are a Swiss couple, who came here in 1990 and swiftly made a name for themselves as producers of weighty but modern-style Séguret and Gigondas.

In Sablet itself, a compact medieval village with some surviving walls and towers, Jean-Marc Autran runs his Domaine de Piaugier in a fairly cramped winery along the road to Gigondas. Autran is a serious young man with a range of serious wines: no fewer than three different single-vineyard Sablets, as well as a Gigondas.

Continue toward Gigondas, which lies above the valley on the lower slopes of the Dentelles. Before you reach the village you will see signs for the reliable Domaine St-Gayan to the right and Domaine les Pallières to the left. This is well worth visiting – an old-fashioned estate, run by an elderly bachelor who has seen so many vintages that he doesn't even bottle his wines until at least five years after the harvest.

Gigondas is the most robust of the Villages wines: deep-coloured, high in alcohol, but balanced with plump, rich Grenache fruit, and was promoted to its own AC in 1971. In good vintages it can keep well for a decade or more. The road up to the village square, which nestles against the hill-side, passes two good domaines, du Gour de Chaulé and du Cayron. The square itself is filled with retail outlets for various estates, but the best place to buy wine is the Caveau du Gigondas, which has the widest range. On the road leading down from the village is the reliable Domaine du Grapillon d'Or, and along the D7 to the right are two very fine estates: Domaine Raspail-Ay, which makes outstanding Gigondas, and Domaine les Goubert, where Jean-Pierre Cartier makes a wide range of wines.

A rising star, the Domaine Santa-Duc, is also located off the D7, in the direction of Vacqueyras. A great place for lunch is Les Florets, a rustic inn high up in the Dentelles. The owner is also proprietor of a wine estate, and old vintages of his excellent Vacqueyras are listed at modest prices.

Several estates in Gigondas, such as Domaine la Fourmone, also produce Vacqueyras but there are fewer good domaines to visit in Vacqueyras, the only other village with its own AC status. Nevertheless, it is worth negotiating the back lanes beyond the church to find Domaine le Clos des Cazaux, which makes delicious wines from both villages. You can taste and buy at the friendly Caveau des Dentelles de Montmirail in the church square.

Take the Carpentras road and you will drive right past the famous Beaumes-de-Venise co-operative or Cave des

The village of Gigondas nestles among low hills against the backdrop of the Dentelles de Montmirail. Grenache is the appellation's major grape variety and it thrives on the area's dry, stony soil.

The lovely Ventoux region is an increasingly successful AC with vineyards on the lower southern slopes of Mont Ventoux.

Vignerons. In the early 1980s its fortified Muscat was all the rage, and the wine is still good: orangy, zesty and invigorating. You can try different wines at the co-operative. The bustling village itself sprawls beneath the castle ruins.

It is only a short distance from Beaumes-de-Venise to Carpentras, but if you wish to return directly to Orange, it is better to take a cross-country short-cut to avoid the traffic snarls around Carpentras. It is, however, a fascinating town, with well-preserved structures from most phases of its long history. In one of the town's main squares, shared by the 17th-century Palais des Justices and the Gothic cathedral, you will find a Roman arch, now somewhat dwarfed by the buildings around it. The cathedral has a richly canopied south door, through which the Jews of Carpentras were driven in an effort to convert them to Christianity. The Jews effectively resisted this pressure and flourished in Carpentras for centuries.

Carpentras is also a good base for exploring the Mont Ventoux region, which is scenically more spectacular than the Côtes du Rhône-Villages, although the wines are considerably less consistent in quality. Until recently the region was dominated by co-operatives, but today there is an increasing number of private estates which are more interested in quality than quantity, such as Ch. Valcombe at St-Pierre-de-Vassols and Domaine des Anges at Mormoiron. A detour through this region also allows you to combine wine-tasting with visits to the delightful villages of Roussillon, Gordes, Fontaine-de-Vaucluse and Crillon-le-Brave, as well as an expedition to Mont Ventoux itself.

Rhône-Villages Fact File

The Côtes du Rhône-Villages region caters admirably to visitors with tasting rooms and sales outlets in the major villages and good, if not outstanding, hotels and restaurants.

Information

Maison des Vins
6 rue des Trois Faucons, 84024 Avignon. Tel 04 90 27 24 00; fax 04 90 27 24 38.
Excellent maps and brochures listing the main wine estates.

Maison du Tourisme et des Vins
Place du Chanoine Sautel, 84110 Vaison-la-Romaine. Tel 04 90 36 02 11.

Office de Tourisme
5 cours Aristide Briand, 84100 Orange. Tel 04 90 34 70 88; fax 04 90 34 99 62.

Musée du Vigneron
D975, 84110 Rasteau. Tel 04 90 46 11 75.
Interesting wine museum owned by the Domaine de Beaurenard in Châteauneuf-du-Pape.

Markets

Carpentras – Friday
Orange – Thursday
Vaison – Tuesday

Festivals and Events

Many villages hold boisterous wine fairs. Rasteau holds its *Fête des Vins* on 14 August, while Séguret has two fairs: in August and December. The *Grand Fête des Côtes du Rhône*, held in Avignon in late November, is more commercial. In Orange the *Foire des Vins* takes place on the last weekend in January.

Where to Buy Wine

In addition to the tasting rooms open at most estates and all co-operatives, there are sales outlets in many wine villages.
Maison Vigneronne
Place des Écoles, 84290 Cairanne. Tel 04 90 30 77 57.
The sales outlet for Domaines Richard and Rabasse-Charavin.

Caveau du Belvedere
Route de Ste-Cécile, 84290 Cairanne. Tel 04 90 30 85 71.

A tasting room and sales outlet for 16 local estates.

Caveau du Gigondas
Place de la Mairie, 84190 Gigondas. Tel 04 90 65 82 29.
A good selection of wines from many of the leading estates.

Caveau des Dentelles de Montmirail
Place de l'Église, Vacqueyras. Tel 04 90 65 86 62.
Open daily with free tastings.

Where to Stay and Eat

Given the abundance of excellent wine in the region, the choice of good establishments is surprisingly restricted.
Arène Ⓗ
Place des Langes, 84100 Orange. Tel 04 90 34 10 95; fax 04 90 34 91 62. ⒻⒻ
In the heart of the city, facing a tranquil little square, this hotel has to be the first choice for visitors to Orange. Parking and garage.

La Beaugravière ⒽⓇ
N7, 84430 Mondragon. Tel 04 90 40 82 54; fax 04 90 40 91 01. ⒻⒻ
This charming restaurant has a dream of a wine list: 200 Châteauneufs, a dozen vintages of Chave's Hermitage, Guigal's rarest wines and Domaine de Trévallon. Prices are amazingly affordable. There are 3 bedrooms.

Hostellerie Beffroi Ⓗ
Rue de l'Évêché, 84110 Vaison-la-Romaine. Tel 04 90 36 04 71; fax 04 90 36 24 78. ⒻⒻ
Beautifully converted 16th-century house in the *ville haute*.

Bellerive Ⓗ
84110 Rasteau. Tel 04 90 46 10 20; fax 04 90 46 14 96. ⒻⒻ
A tranquil hotel with splendid views of Mont Ventoux.

Burrhus Ⓗ
1 place Monfort, 84110 Vaison-la-Romaine. Tel 04 90 36 00 11;

fax 04 90 36 39 05. Ⓕ
An unusually stylish hotel on the main square.

Auberge de Cabasse ⒽⓇ
84110 Séguret. Tel 04 90 46 91 12; fax 04 90 46 94 01. ⒻⒻ
Small inn belonging to a good wine estate. The terraces and swimming pool make this an excellent base.

La Fête en Provence Ⓡ
Place du Vieux-Marché, 84110 Vaison-la-Romaine. Tel 04 90 36 36 43; fax 04 90 36 21 49. ⒻⒻ
Lively restaurant with summer terrace and busy in season. Strongly flavoured cooking and inexpensive wines.

Les Florets ⒽⓇ
Route des Dentelles de Montmirail, 84190 Gigondas. Tel 04 90 65 85 01; fax 04 90 65 83 80. Ⓕ
Rustic but comfortable inn in mountain scenery. Sound food, but the main attraction is the delicious wines made by the owner, Thierry Bernard, as well as old Gigondas and Vacqueyras wines at bargain prices.

Le Forum Ⓡ
3 rue Mazeau, 84100 Orange. Tel 04 90 34 01 09. Ⓕ
Modest but reliable cooking.

Le Glacier Ⓗ
48 cours Aristide Briand, 84100 Orange. Tel 04 90 34 02 01; fax 04 90 51 13 80. Ⓕ
Pleasant and comfortable rooms.

Au Gout de Jour Ⓡ
9 place aux Herbes, 84100 Orange. Tel 04 90 34 10 80. Ⓕ
Attractive and unpretentious restaurant in the middle of the old town.

Le Logis du Château ⒽⓇ
Les Hauts de Vaison, 84100 Vaison-la-Romaine. Tel 04 90 36 09 98; fax 04 90 36 10 95. ⒻⒻ
Vaison is often overrun with tourists in high season, but this pleasant hotel is tranquil and close to the town.

Le Mas des Aigras (H)
Chemin des Aigras, 84100
Orange. Tel 04 90 34 81 01;
fax 04 90 34 05 66. (F)(F)
Rural calm on the outskirts of
Orange in a converted Provençal
farmhouse.

Mas de Bouvau (R)
Route de Cairanne, 84150
Violès. Tel 04 90 70 94 08;
fax 04 90 70 95 99. (F)(F)
Straightforward cooking with
Provençal touches in a former
farmhouse. Fairly pricy wine list.

Le Parvis (R)
3 cours Pourtoules, 84100
Orange. Tel 04 90 34 82 00. (F)
Ambitious Provençal restaurant
located behind the Roman
theatre. Fish, rabbit and pigeon
often feature on the menu.

La Table du Comtat (H)(R)
84110 Séguret. Tel 04 90 46 91
49; fax 04 90 46 94 27. (F)(F)
This establishment enjoys
ravishing views from the top of
the picturesque village. There are
small, pretty rooms and an

attractive swimming pool. The
restaurant serves accomplished
and generous cooking and has an
excellent wine list, particularly
strong in Rhône wines.

Hostellerie du Vieux Château
(H)(R)
Route Ste-Cécile, 84830 Sérignan-
du-Comtat. Tel 04 90 70 05 58;
fax 04 90 70 05 62. (F)(F)
An 18th-century farmhouse with
a shady garden and small pool.
Pleasant restaurant with well-
chosen local wines.

Wines and Wine Villages

The Côtes du Rhône AC accounts for 85 per cent of all
southern Rhône AC wines. The top 16 villages have Côtes
du Rhône-Villages status, and two of the best, Gigondas
and Vacqueyras, now have their own ACs. Red and white
Grenache are the main grape varieties.

Beaumes-de-Venise Famous
for its sweet Muscat wine, this
attractive village is also a good
producer of red Côtes du
Rhône-Villages with ripe,
plummy fruit in warm years.
*Best producers: Cave des
Vignerons,* LES GOUBERT, *Pascal.*

Cairanne These ancient
vineyards, first planted in the
Middle Ages, today encompass
both the slopes and the more
gravelly and sandy plateau below.
Quality varies, but the best
estates produce red wines of
power and finesse as well as
flavoursome whites, suggesting
that the full potential of
Cairanne has yet to be realized.
The village is a delight.
Best producers: CAVE DE
CAIRANNE, L'ORATOIRE ST-MARTIN,
Rabasse-Charavin, Richaud.

Chusclan One of the Villages
in the Gard department. Once
celebrated for rosé, today reds
account for most of the
production. Drink the wines
young, while they retain their
youthful fruit.
Best producer: Lindas.

Côtes du Rhône AC The
general AC for the whole
Rhône Valley but most of the

wine comes from the southern
part. Over 90 per cent are red or
rosé, mainly from Grenache with
some Cinsaut, Syrah, Carignan
and Mourvèdre to add lots of
warm, spicy southern personality.
Modern wine-making has
revolutionized the style and
today's wines are generally juicy,
spicy and easy to drink. Most
wine is made by the co-operatives
and sold under merchants' labels.
The pure Syrah from Ch. de
Fonsalette is the outstanding
wine of the appellation, but it is
rare and very expensive.
*Best producers: l'Estagnol, de
Fonsalette, Grand Moulas, du
Roure, St-Estève d'Uchaux, St-
Apollinaire, Treilles, Vieille Ferme.*

Côtes du Rhône-Villages AC
This AC is for wines with a
higher minimum alcohol content
than Côtes du Rhône. A total of
16 villages in the southern
Rhône that have traditionally
made superior wine are entitled
to add their name to the AC,
with a further 54 villages allowed
to use the AC without any
specific village name on the
label. Almost all the wine is red
and it can have a marvellous
spicy flavour.
For best producers see individual
village entries in this section.

Côtes du Ventoux AC A
large region overshadowed by
Mont Ventoux. Long dominated
by co-operatives, the AC is
finally showing the quality of
which it is capable, although its
wines still lack a clear identity.
*Best producers: Anges, Crillon,
Jaboulet, Pascal, Vieille Ferme,
Vieux-Lazaret.*

Gigondas AC Few would
dispute that Gigondas produces
the mightiest red wine of the
Villages region and the village
was promoted from Rhône-
Villages to its own AC in 1971.
Grenache is the main grape and
the very hot mesoclimate usually
delivers powerful wines that can
easily attain 14 degrees of
alcohol. A few producers have
experimented with oaked wines,
which have found favour with
American wine lovers but are
decried locally as atypical.
Indeed, Gigondas scarcely seems
to require additional tannins
from oak barrels. Except in light
vintages such as 1992, Gigondas
should be aged 5 years or more
to be enjoyed at its best.
Best producers: Cayron, LE CLOS
DES CAZAUX, LES GOUBERT, *du
Gour de Chaulé, du Grapillon d'Or,*
PALLIÈRES, RASPAIL-AY, *St-Gayan,*
SANTA-DUC.

Laudun A Village in the Gard
department, with vineyards
planted on gravelly soils. With
very few exceptions the wines
are light and lack depth of
flavour. They should be drunk

within 3 years, when they can be most enjoyable.
Best producers: Pélaquié, Serre-Biau.

Muscat de Beaumes-de-Venise VDN A delicious and highly fragrant sweet golden wine, this Muscat is justifiably popular. At the excellent co-operative you can taste different qualities and judge which style you find most attractive. Drink the wine chilled.
Best producers: Cave des Vignerons, Durban, Jaboulet, Vidal-Fleury.

Rasteau VDN If any Village deserves to join Gigondas and Vacqueyras as a full-blown AC on its own, then it is probably Rasteau, which can produce powerful, peppery and long-lived reds. The local speciality is Vin Doux Naturel, a fortified Grenache wine. Some producers dislike it, feeling their best Grenache grapes should be reserved for the reds.
Best producers: (red and VDN) Bressy-Masson, Cave des Vignerons, DE LA SOUMADE; *(red only)* LES GOUBERT, Rabasse-Charavin.

Roaix A little-known Village that once constituted part of the papal vineyards. The vineyard area is a mere 43ha, so the wines are rarely found and the zone is allied through the co-operative with neighbouring Séguret.
Best producers: Roaix co-operative.

Rochegude A small Village north of Orange made famous when Thomas Jefferson recommended its wines to George Washington. They are mostly made by the co-operative.

Rousset-les-Vignes In the north of the region, within the Drôme department, this small Villages zone produces somewhat tannic red wines that often benefit from some bottle age. The village has a fine Renaissance château.
Best producer: Union des Producteurs.

Sablet These vineyards adjoin those of Gigondas and can sometimes rival it in quality. This

Domaine de Cabasse's vineyards are below the village of Séguret.

is one of the few Villages with a deserved reputation for well-structured white wines, too.
Best producers: LES GOUBERT, DE PIAUGIER.

St-Gervais One of 3 Rhône-Villages in the Gard department, with very varied soils. The reds, made with ample Mourvèdre, can be sappy and stylish and deserve to be better known, as do the rosés. Good value.
Best producers: Clavel, Ste-Anne.

St-Maurice-sur-Eygues An obscure Village in the Drôme whose reds develop considerable finesse with some bottle-aging.
Best producers: Cave de St-Maurice, de Deurre.

St-Pantaléon-les-Vignes A little-known Village in the Drôme, where the co-operative produces gutsy reds from here and from Rousset-les-Vignes.
Best producer: Union des Producteurs.

Séguret This is the best-preserved medieval village in the southern Rhône, and the wines are attractive, too: full-flavoured reds with good acidity and robust whites.
Best producers: DE L'AMANDINE, DE CABASSE, Couranconne.

Vacqueyras AC Promoted to AC status in 1990, Vacqueyras is making a direct challenge to the

supremacy of Gigondas, even though the same producers tend to make both wines. Robust, but less structured than Gigondas, these are reds to drink about 5 years after the vintage. The whites and rosés still lag far behind in terms of quality.
Best producers: LE CLOS DES CAZAUX, la Fourmone, la Garrigue, Sang des Cailloux.

Valréas Sitting on hill in an isolated part of the Vaucluse, Valréas is, in fact, a small enclave within the Drôme department. The wines, both red and white, deserve to be better known. The village even has a museum on the history of the cardboard box!
Best producers: Grands Devers, Val des Rois.

Vinsobres A large zone within the Drôme, producing reds that are often full-bodied, quite high in acidity and long-lived. Most estates are located on the terraces below the village.
Best producers: Aussellons, de Deurre.

Visan Like Valréas, Visan was once part of the papal vineyards located within the Drôme department. It is better known for its truffles than for its wines. The reds are fruity and powerful, but the rosés and whites have a less well-defined character.
Best producers: Cantharide, Cave des Coteaux.

Like Bordeaux, Châteauneuf-du-Pape is a region of many large estates, most of which are of one piece with the vineyards surrounding the château and its outbuildings. With such a wide choice of grape varieties, soils and vinification methods, the styles of wine from the top estates contrast interestingly with one another. This is Ch. de Beaucastel owned by the Perrin family. It is one of the largest and best properties in the AC and also one of the most ancient, with records dating back to the 16th century. Located in the north-east of Châteauneuf-du-Pape, near Courthézon, de Beaucastel's vineyards are on clayey-sandy soil which has a high proportion of the famous Châteauneuf stones or *galets*. The young vines are bush-trained against wooden stakes to help protect them from the Mistral wind which roars across the Châteauneuf plateau for up to 120 days a year. Unlike most estates, de Beaucastel grows all 13 permitted Châteauneuf varieties, with Grenache Noir and Mourvèdre the dominant ones. The vineyards are run on organic lines.

From Ch. Fortia's vineyards there is a good view of the ruined 14th-century papal castle that dominates the village of Châteauneuf-du-Pape.

Châteauneuf-du-Pape, Tavel & Lirac

Thanks to its ancient papal patronage, Châteauneuf-du-Pape has long been one of the most celebrated wines of France. It comes from an awe-inspiring plateau strewn with large stones, called *galets*, that radiate heat on summer nights, elevating the grapes' sugar content to extremes of potency. There is little here other than vines and a ruined château, but Châteauneuf and its neighbouring appellations of Lirac and Tavel lie close to the glorious city of Avignon.

The Tour

It makes sense to begin any exploration of Châteauneuf-du-Pape in Avignon, for it was here that the papal court settled in the 14th century. Cut off from its former sources of wine in Italy, the court turned instead to the splendid wine region immediately north of the city. Pope Clement V would make personal inspection tours of the vineyards, checking on the health of his vines. His successor John XXII built the castle at Châteauneuf and used it as a summer residence. A few decades ago there was a good deal of bogus Châteauneuf on the market, and in order to uphold the reputation of their wines the local producers clamped down on such fraudulent practices. Today estate-bottled Châteauneuf wines have the papal coat of arms embossed on the heavy glass bottle – an impressive marketing strategy to guarantee their authenticity – and the reputation of the wines has been restored, along with the fairly high prices.

Avignon is ringed by high walls, and there is ample parking beneath them, although, as everywhere in tourist-thronged southern France, the summer months bring huge crowds. This magnificent little city still conveys its medieval might with effortless ease. At the highest corner of the old city you will find the major buildings: the cathedral, the Papal Palace and the Petit Palais.

The 12th-century cathedral pre-dates the Papal Palace, but there is little to see inside it other than the imposing 13th-century bishop's chair. Other fine buildings cluster around the palace: the Mint, its blank wall encrusted with stone swags, coats of arms and inscriptions; and the Petit Palais, which could easily be mistaken for a transplanted Oxford college. This handsome building, with its fine Gothic courtyard, houses a huge collection of medieval Italian paintings, as well as paintings and sculpture produced in Avignon between the 12th and 15th centuries.

There is much more to enjoy in Avignon, such as the rue des Tenturiers, where the houses are reached by bridges

TOUR SUMMARY

This is a circular tour, beginning and ending in Avignon. It takes you to the most important wine estates in Châteauneuf and then on to Tavel, with its fine rosé wine, and to neighbouring Lirac, which produces good red wines as well.

Distance covered   The distance covered is not great: 100km (60 miles).

Time needed   1 day.

Terrain   Driving is easy around Châteauneuf-du-Pape and the area consists of a flat, feature-less sandy plateau covered in large stones, or *galets*, that absorb heat from the sun during the day and radiate it at night.

Hotels   There are few hotels on this tour except for those in or near Avignon, where there is a wide choice at all price levels.

Restaurants   Apart from the excellent la Sommellerie near Châteauneuf, those in search of fine cooking will find it only in or around Avignon, which also offers a wide selection of wine bars and restaurants. There are simpler establishments in Châteauneuf itself and in Tavel.

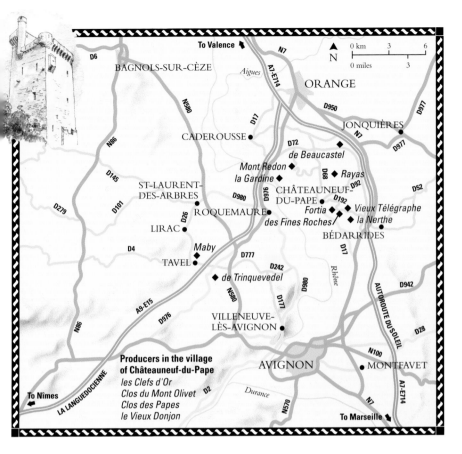

To Valence

N7

BAGNOLS-SUR-CÈZE *Aigues*

ORANGE

0 km 3 6
0 miles 3
N

D6

N580

D17

D950

D977

CADEROUSSE ●

D72

JONQUIÈRES

N7

D977

de Beaucastel ◆

N86

Mont Redon ◆

la Gardine ◆

D68 ◆ Rayas

D145

ST-LAURENT-
DES-ARBRES

CHÂTEAUNEUF-
DU-PAPE ●

D92

D52

D980

D976

D192

D279

D101

ROQUEMAURE ●

D26

Fortia ◆ ◆ Vieux Télégraphe

des Fines Roches / ◆ la Nerthe

LIRAC ●

BÉDARRIDES

D4

Maby ◆

D17

TAVEL ●

D777

D242

◆ de Trinquevedel

D980

D171

Rhône

D942

N580

AUTOROUTE DU SOLEIL

D28

N86

A9-E15

D976

VILLENEUVE-
LÈS-AVIGNON ●

N100

**Producers in the village
of Châteauneuf-du-Pape**
*les Clefs d'Or
Clos du Mont Olivet*
*Clos des Papes
le Vieux Donjon*

AVIGNON

● MONTFAVET

A7-E714

LA LANGUEDOCIENNE

To Nîmes

D2

Durance

N570

N7

To Marseille

across the tiny Sorgue river. There is another attractive district around the Place Carnot behind the Place de l'Horloge, where you will find the main market – les Halles – the neo-classical synagogue and the flamboyant Gothic church of St-Pierre.

But it is the mighty fortress-like Papal Palace that is the main attraction. The immense scale of the halls and chapels demonstrate that they were intended for display, for conclaves and banquets. Don't miss the Hall of the Consistory, with its fascinating frescos by Simone Martini. The great Sienese painter was summoned here in 1340 and executed these frescos for the cathedral porch, but they have since been moved into the palace. The papal bedrooms are also beautifully decorated with charming frescos.

It will take no more than half an hour to reach Châteauneuf-du-Pape from Avignon. Just before you reach the outskirts of the city on the D17, you will see signs for Ch. Fortia. It's worth pausing here, not only because the wine is good but because this was where the reputation of Châteauneuf was revived. Fortia was, indeed still is, the home of the Le Roy family, and in 1923 Baron Le Roy, exasperated by the adulteration of this once-famous wine, devised a charter that would maintain quality by specifying

Map illustration: the medieval tower in the village of Lirac.

permitted grape varieties, outlawing the production of rosé and insisting on a minimum alcohol level of 12.5 degrees, the highest in France. The charter is still in effect.

No fewer than 13 grape varieties are permitted in Châteauneuf, and a few domaines, such as de Beaucastel, use all of them. But Grenache is the dominant variety, and it is ideally suited to the stony vineyards, soaking up the summer sunshine, and the stored nocturnal heat from the fist-sized *galets*. (To see the quintessential Châteauneuf landscape, take the D68 road toward Orange and turn left to Ch. Mont Redon, across the plateau, which is studded with *galets*.)

Only in Châteauneuf does Grenache achieve such splendour and longevity, and these days the wine lover is spoiled for choice since there is an abundance of excellent estates. The white wine is delicious, too – more expensive than the red because of its scarcity – and it can be enjoyed very young, when it is explosively fruity, or after about eight years in bottle, when it has developed complex secondary aromas.

On the way into the village of Châteauneuf from Avignon you will pass Domaine Clos des Papes on your right. Paul Avril and his son Vincent have long produced an extremely consistent wine, carefully blending lots from their 17 vineyards. Few growers know more about the region and its wines than the Avrils, and if they are not too preoccupied with work in the vineyard or winery, they will be only too happy to talk to you. Their wines are relatively expensive, but worth it.

In the heart of Châteauneuf itself is a fountain where the town elders congregate for a gossip. Next to it is the very helpful Office de Tourisme and, opposite, the narrow rue Joseph Ducos rises up to the ruined papal castle, now sufficiently patched up to allow banquets and other events to be held there. Two of the village's restaurants, la Garbure and le Pistou, are located on this street.

The road to Bédarrides leads to Ch. la Nerthe and, right at the edge of the appellation, to the celebrated Domaine Vieux Télégraphe. La Nerthe is of interest because it is one of the few estates to age some of its wines in new oak. The oaked red, Cuvée des Cadettes, is made from vines up to a century old. A white Cuvée, Clos de Beauvenir, gets similar treatment. You can also find oaked Châteauneuf at Ch. la Gardine. Not everyone likes these wines, and they are extremely expensive, but they are worth trying.

Vieux Télégraphe is a deservedly popular wine. Unlike some, the estate is well equipped and makes good wines in lesser vintages, too. It is characterized by rich fruit and is more approachable young than some more traditional wines from the region.

The Châteauneuf-du-Pape vineyards contain a wide variety of soils but most famous of all is the stony plateau in the north around Courthézon where the large white pebbles, or galets roulés, *cover the soil completely. These pebbles store daytime heat, which is then radiated back onto the vines at night, as well as absorbing valuable moisture.*

Back in Châteauneuf, alongside the D17 road, is a cluster of far more traditional estates: le Vieux Donjon, Clos du Mont Olivet and les Clefs d'Or. All produce dark, robust wines of great concentration that easily keep for a decade or more. There is little to see in the way of cellars, but there are always wines open for tasting and a warm welcome.

You can either remain in Châteauneuf for lunch or head out to La Sommellerie on the D17 road to Roquemaure. Apart from the rather formal Ch. des Fines Roches, this is the only option in the region for distinguished and innovative cooking, and the poolside setting among the vines is especially delightful in summer. The *sommelier* is excellent.

It is tempting to direct visitors to the most famous of all Châteauneuf estates, Ch. Rayas. But there is little point. It is hard to find, and visitors, even those from the wine trade with appointments, are scarcely made welcome. The owner, Jacques Reynaud, has been known to hide in the bushes rather than receive a visitor. Nonetheless, the wines can be magnificent, if inconsistent.

Your time is better spent visiting Ch. de Beaucastel, north of the village of Châteauneuf and alongside the A7-E714 *autoroute*. If consistency and longevity are indicators of quality, then de Beaucastel can claim to be Châteauneuf's best estate. Using all permitted grape varieties, including a substantial amount of Mourvèdre, de Beaucastel never lets you down. The estate is located in the flattest corner of the region and there is little to see, but one must pay homage to a wine that, in its white as well as red incarnations, gives such profound pleasure.

These new oak barrels at Ch. la Nerthe are just one sign of recent investment in the vineyards and cellars. Under new owners, this leading Châteauneuf-du-Pape estate is now undergoing a much-needed renaissance.

If you enjoy the robustness of Châteauneuf, you will also be impressed by two neighbouring appellations, Tavel and Lirac. Lirac produces rosé, as well as red and white wines, but Tavel is one of the few ACs dedicated exclusively to rosé. Both are easy to reach from Châteauneuf. Take the D976 road to Roquemaure, and then follow it southward toward Nîmes. The village of Tavel is on the right, but its leading estate, Ch. de Trinquevedel, lies to the left of the main road.

Although machine-harvesting is permitted, all grapes are picked by hand at de Trinquevedel, and white as well as red grapes are used to make the wine. Tavel is an acquired taste: it is always dry and quite high in alcohol and is best drunk with food. Tavel can be aged, and M. Demoulin, the present proprietor of this fine 18th-century château, recommends that it be drunk at between two and four years old.

Although Domaine Maby is based in the village of Tavel, it is better known for its excellent Lirac. The red is a well-structured wine, capable of aging, which is typical of the appellation in being slightly less powerful than Châteauneuf but with greater finesse.

From Tavel it is only a short drive back to Avignon.

Châteauneuf-du-Pape, Tavel & Lirac Fact File

Avoid staying in Châteauneuf itself because of the parking problem. The Ch. des Fines Roches is an attractive but pricy option, but Avignon offers a wide choice.

Information

Office de Tourisme
Place du Portail, 84230 Châteauneuf-du-Pape. Tel 04 90 83 72 21; fax 04 90 93 50 34.

Maison des Vins
6 rue des Trois Faucons, 84024 Avignon. Tel 04 90 27 24 00; fax 04 90 27 24 38. Excellent maps and brochures listing the main wine estates.

Musée des Outils de Vignerons
Caves Brotte, 84230 Châteauneuf-du-Pape. Tel 04 90 83 70 07; fax 04 90 83 74 34. An interesting wine museum and free tasting of wines from the *négociant* Père Anselme.

Markets
Avignon – daily
Châteauneuf-du-Pape – Friday

Festivals and Events
The main wine festival in Châteauneuf is the *Fête de la Véraison* during the first weekend in August. There are free tastings as well as folkloric events to celebrate the reddening of the ripening grapes. The *St-Marc* festival on 25 April consists of processions and wine-judging. Larger, more commercial wine festivals are held in Avignon in late November at the *Grand Fête des Côtes du Rhône* (tel 04 90 27 24 14 for information).

Where to Buy Wine
La Coupe d'Or
Place Jerusalem, 84000 Avignon. Tel 04 90 82 18 31. Good source of local wines as well as Burgundy and Bordeaux.

Prestige et Tradition
3 rue de la République, 84230 Châteauneuf-du-Pape. Tel 04 90 83 72 29. Bottling and sales outlet for a group of Châteauneuf producers, including the reliable Bosquet des Papes, Dom. de la Solitude and le Vieux Donjon.

Cave Reflets
3 chemin du Bois de la Ville, 84230 Châteauneuf-du-Pape. Tel 0490 83 71 07. Bottling and sales outlet for the excellent estates of les Cailloux, Clos du Mont Olivet, Chante Perdrix and others. Beware of older vintages which may have been kept in cask too long.

Caveau St-Vincent
30126 Tavel. Tel 04 66 50 24 10.

Where to Stay and Eat
Most of the best restaurants are found in or around Avignon.
Christian Étienne ®
10-12 rue de Mons, 84000 Avignon. Tel 04 90 86 16 50; fax 04 90 86 67 09. Ⓕ Ⓕ Outstanding restaurant serving superlative vegetables and fish. Excellent wine list.

The papal coat of arms of Châteauneuf-du-Pape indicates wine bottled by the estate.

Château des Fines Roches Ⓗ ®
Route de Sorgues, 84230 Châteauneuf-du-Pape. Tel 04 90 83 70 23; fax 04 90 83 78 42. Ⓕ Ⓕ Dominating the surrounding vineyards this grand château serves good, sensibly priced food in a rather formal atmosphere.

Château de Cubières ®
30150 Roquemaure. Tel 04 66 82 89 33; fax 04 66 82 60 04. Ⓕ Ⓕ Good cooking served in a delightful 18th-century château.

Les Frênes Ⓗ ®
645 avenue Vertes-Rives, 84000 Montfavet. Tel 04 90 31 17 93; fax 04 90 23 95 03. Ⓕ Ⓕ Ⓕ Comfortable, tranquil country house in a sumptuous setting. The luxurious restaurant has a fine selection of Rhône wines.

La Garbure Ⓗ ®
Rue Joseph Ducos, 84230 Châteauneuf-du-Pape. Tel 04 90 83 75 08; fax 04 90 83 52 34. Ⓕ The 'Menu Suggestion' offers fresh local produce, served in a pretty little dining room. Simple rooms available.

Le Grangousier ®
17 rue Galante, 84000 Avignon. Tel 04 90 82 96 60; fax 04 90 85 31 23. Ⓕ Ⓕ A rising star in Avignon, offering the finest food in a smart setting at affordable prices.

Hiély-Lucullus ®
5 rue de la République, 84000 Avignon. Tel 04 90 86 17 07; fax 04 90 86 32 38. Ⓕ Ⓕ For many years Avignon's gastronomic temple but now facing formidable competition. This still notable restaurant is best known for its excellent fish dishes. Good but pricy wine list.

L'Isle Sonnante ®
7 rue Racine, 84000 Avignon. Tel 04 90 82 56 01. Ⓕ Ⓕ Another of Avignon's excellent restaurants. Very good wine list.

Le Jardin de la Tour ®
9 rue de la Tour, 84000 Avignon. Tel 04 90 85 66 50; fax 04 90 27 90 72. Ⓕ Ⓕ Attractive, with a shady courtyard; offers simply prepared classics of Provençal cooking.

Hôtel Mediéval Ⓗ
15 rue Petite-Saunerie, 84000 Avignon. Tel 04 90 86 11 06; fax 04 90 82 08 64. Ⓕ Small hotel in a 17th-century house near the Papal Palace.

Le Pistou ®
15 rue Joseph Ducos, 84230 Châteauneuf-du-Pape.

Tel 04 90 83 71 75. **Ⓕ**
Flavourful Provençal cooking.

Le Prieuré Ⓗ Ⓡ
7 place du Chapitre, 30400
Villeneuve-lès-Avignon. Tel 04
90 25 18 20; fax 04 90 25 45 39.
Ⓕ Ⓕ
Exquisite comfort in a medieval
priory with lovely gardens. First-
rate classic food, served on a
terrace in summer, and wine list.

La Sommellerie Ⓡ
Route de Roquemaure, 84230
Châteauneuf-du-Pape. Tel 04 90
83 50 00; fax 04 90 83 51 85.
Ⓕ Ⓕ
Ambitious food and a splendid
wine list.

Auberge de Tavel Ⓗ Ⓡ
Voie Romaine, 30126 Tavel.
Tel 04 66 50 03 41; fax 04 66 50
24 44. **Ⓕ Ⓕ**

Comfortable but quite expensive
hotel. The menus offered by the
welcoming restaurant feature
some regional dishes. Pricy local
wine list.

Les Trois Clefs Ⓡ
26 rue des Trois Faucons, 84000
Avignon. Tel 04 90 86 51 53;
fax 04 90 85 17 32. **Ⓕ**
Stylish restaurant serving good
Côtes du Rhône wines.

Wines and Wine Villages

Châteauneuf, with its ruined papal castle, dominates the
landscape while the upper part of the village is charming.
Tavel is also an enjoyable place to visit.

Châteauneuf-du-Pape AC
This celebrated wine has had its
ups and down over the decades,
but is now back on top form.
Always choose an estate wine,
distinguished by the papal coat of
arms embossed on the neck of
the bottle. The red is not for the
faint-hearted – 13 grape varieties
are authorized and Grenache, the
dominant grape, flourishes on
Châteauneuf's stony soils,
sometimes attaining 15 degrees
of alcohol. Some estates try to
achieve greater finesse by using a
fair proportion of Syrah or
Mourvèdre, or by aging part of
the wine in barriques. Some
large, modern-style estates, such
as Mont Redon, have lightened
their style, but at a risk of the
loss of typicity. Others remain
doggedly traditional, producing
massively structured wines
intended for long aging.

Serious efforts are being
made to produce outstanding
whites from Roussanne and
other varieties. Cooler years,
which give lighter reds atypical
of the AC, are often excellent
white wine vintages. The whites
can either be drunk young, when
flowery and fresh, or aged for 7
or 8 years, when the best attain a
surprising depth and complexity.
Best producers: DE BEAUCASTEL,
Bonneau, Chapoutier 'Barberac', les
Clefs d'Or, CLOS DU MONT OLIVET,

*Many Lirac vineyards are covered in a
stony surface similar to that of nearby
Châteauneuf-du-Pape.*

CLOS DES PAPES, FORTIA, *Janasse,*
LA NERTHE, *Pegaü,* RAYAS, *Sabon,*
LE VIEUX DONJON, VIEUX
TÉLÉGRAPHE.

Lirac AC The 1200ha of
vineyards are divided among
4 villages, of which the most
important are Lirac itself and
Roquemaure. Most of the
production is red wine, but
25 per cent is rosé and 10 per
cent white. Although the soil
resembles Châteauneuf's, the
wines are lighter and often more
elegant. Nonetheless, they are
very much wines of the South,
and can pack quite a punch.
Quality remains variable, and it
is best to taste before you buy.

At its best, red Lirac is very
good value. The whites and
rosés tend to be less interesting.
Best producers: *Aquéria,* MABY,
Mordorée, St-Roch.

Tavel AC This is a unique AC
in that its entire production from
870ha of vineyards is rosé wine.
White grapes, as well as traditional
red ones such as Grenache,
Cinsaut and Syrah, are often used
in the blend.

Tavel is full-bodied and very
dry, and most producers block
the malolactic fermentation to
prevent the wines from
becoming too heavy. With
alcohol levels at about 13
degrees, Tavel demands respect
and is best enjoyed with food. It
is often said that Tavel improves
with age. This is debatable, but a
well-made example will certainly
keep for up to 4 years without
deterioration.

With its broad main street,
pleasant hotels and restaurants
and attractive shops, the tiny
village of Tavel is a useful place
to visit. The co-operative
produces over half the wine.
Best producers: *Aquéria,
Forcadière, Genestière,* MABY,
Mordorée, DE TRINQUEVEDEL.

Perched on top of the limestone crags of the Alpilles, the village of les Baux is a major tourist attraction.

Map illustrations: (left) St-Gilles abbey; (centre) lavender, a major local crop; (right) the Moulin de Daudet at Fontvieille is a rare windmill left in Provence today.

Les Baux and Costières de Nîmes

The Rhône separates the two very different wine regions of les Baux-de-Provence and Costières de Nîmes, both struggling to find an identity but producing some remarkable wines. Les Baux is set in one of the wildest landscapes of southern France: the limestone crags of the Alpilles. On their slopes, beneath the abandoned fortress, are planted olive trees and vines. The Costières is a more sprawling region between the Roman city of Nîmes and the watery expanses of the Camargue.

The Tour

This tour, rich in Roman ruins, begins in Arles, a Roman port, which boasts a magnificent amphitheatre. Later Arles became a centre of early Christianity and, in the 9th and 10th centuries, the capital of Provence. The main square, the place de la République, is dominated by the cathedral of

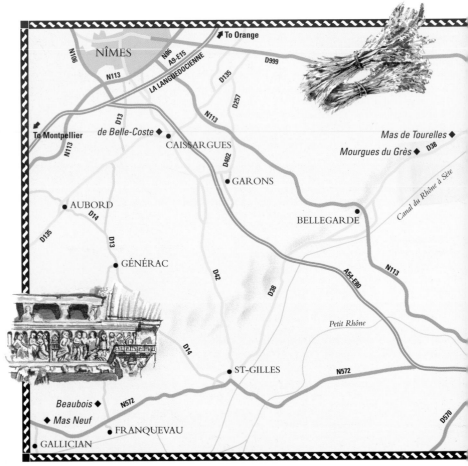

St-Trophime, with its tall belfry and exquisite cloister. It's also worth visiting the Alyscamps, the Roman necropolis.

From Arles, head north-east on the D17 to Fontvieille. You will pass the mighty and exceedingly austere abbey of Montmajour on the right; as remarkable is the exquisite cemetery chapel of Ste-Croix nearby. Fontvieille's chief claim to fame is the Moulin de Daudet, where in 1869 Alphonse Daudet recorded the miller's anecdotes in his ever-popular *Lettres de Mon Moulin*. Today the mill is a museum.

Continue on the D17 to Maussane-les-Alpilles and bear left on the D5. After 2km (1 mile) there is a turning left to les Baux. Do not take it, but continue on the St-Rémy road to Mas de la Dame, the oldest wine estate in the area, which produces wines of a consistently reliable standard. You can also buy excellent olive oil and tapenade here. Return to the crossroads and take the les Baux road, which ascends the Alpilles. You will pass Mas Ste-Berthe, an attractive estate that produces good but rather unexciting wines.

Les Baux is one of the most visited sites in Provence. From its lofty citadel, the local warlords dominated the region in the 12th and 13th centuries; by the 16th century

TOUR SUMMARY

This tour begins in Arles, then takes in the remarkable rocky outcrop of les Baux and estates bordering the mysterious watery region of the Camargue, before ending in Nîmes.

Distance covered   150km (90 miles)

Time needed   1 day

Terrain   The Rhône plain near Arles is broken by the jagged limestone chain of the Alpilles, which rises to some 400m (1300ft). Near the Camargue – the marshy land of the Rhône delta – the landscape again becomes flat.

Hotels   There are wonderful hotels in les Baux and several good ones in Arles, Nîmes and St-Rémy.

Restaurants   Les Baux is one of the gastronomic centres of France and there are other good restaurants throughout the rest of the region.

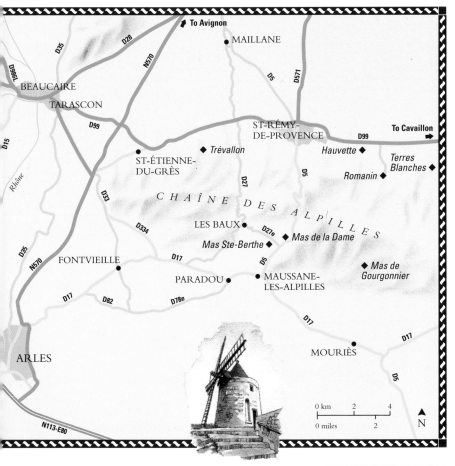

it was a Protestant stronghold. The always rebellious town was stormed and largely destroyed by Cardinal Richelieu in 1632. Until the 1970s les Baux was left undisturbed, but since then much of the town has been reconstructed and filled with souvenir shops, fast-food stalls and mediocre museums.

Follow the D27 toward Maillane and you soon reach the Cathédral d'Images, an audiovisual extravaganza burrowed into the limestone hills. Here, too, is the Maison des Vins, representing 13 properties. This is the place to taste wines from two fine estates that are difficult to find: Mas de Gourgonnier and Domaine Hauvette. Unfortunately, les Baux's greatest wine, Domaine de Trévallon, is not served here, since its blend of Cabernet and Syrah has been ruled out of order by the AC authorities. Follow signs to St-Rémy, drive through the town and take the D5 to the fascinating Roman remains called les Antiques and Glanum.

Return to St-Rémy and take the D99 toward Cavaillon. After a couple of kilometres turn right to Ch. Romanin, an estate run on biodynamic principles which are based on mystical writings by the educator, Rudolf Steiner. The cathedral-like cellars are built into the rock, and bottles are stacked so as to benefit from magnetic forces. Despite the huge investment, the wines are not yet exceptional. Also along the D99 is the organic Domaine des Terres Blanches, which from time to time releases excellent special varietal wines from either Syrah or Cabernet Sauvignon.

Return to St-Rémy, take the D99 and follow signs for Tarascon; cross the Rhône to Beaucaire, then take the D38 toward Bellegarde. You are now in the Costières de Nîmes, a large and increasingly dynamic region, especially for red wines, and now for whites, too. Be sure to stop at the Mas des Tourelles, where the owners have reconstructed a Roman winery, which is in working order and producing wines according to Roman recipes. Further along the D38 is Ch. Mourgues du Grès, which makes delicious reds.

Carry on to St-Gilles, then take the N572 to Gallician and Ch. Mas Neuf, owned by the ebullient Olivier Gibelin. His wines may not be the finest in the region, but they are surely the best value. From the winery you can see the swampy Camargue, famous for its bulls, salt pans and gypsy festivals. Drive back on the N572 to Franquevau and turn left toward Générac. You soon come to Ch. Beaubois, a good source of attractive wines, especially the Cuvée Elegance. Continue to Générac, Aubord and Caissargues, where you will find the Ch. de Belle-Coste. The historic château here is, sadly, in a dilapidated condition but Bertrand du Tremblay's wines, especially the Cuvée St-Marc, are very stylish.

You are now close to Nîmes, where you could enjoy a good meal, spend the night, and visit its Roman sites.

Mas de la Dame is the oldest wine estate in the les Baux AC and is superbly situated on the southern side of the Alpilles.

Les Baux and Costières de Nîmes Fact File

It is rare in rural France to find such a concentration of good hotels and restaurants – and fine wine.

Information

Comité Départemental du Tourisme du Gard
3 place des Arènes, 30011 Nîmes. Tel 04 66 36 96 30; fax 04 66 36 13 14.

Cave et Vins Gallo-Romains
Mas de Tourelles, 4294 route de Bellegarde, 30300 Beaucaire. Tel 04 66 59 19 72; fax 04 66 59 50 80.
Fascinating reconstruction of a working Roman winery and you can taste and buy the unique wines.

Markets

Nîmes, avenue Jean Jaurès – daily
St-Rémy – Wednesday

Festivals and Events

Nîmes has a *Feria des Vendanges* the last weekend of September.

Where to Buy Wine

Maison des Vins
Grande Rue, 13520 les Baux. Tel 06 08 40 48 75.
Wines from all the les Baux estates, except for de Trévallon.

Where to Stay and Eat

Le Cabro d'Or Ⓗ Ⓡ
Val d'Enfer, 13520 les Baux. Tel 04 90 54 33 21; fax 04 90 54 45 98. Ⓕ Ⓕ Ⓕ

In the same ownership as l'Oustau de Baumanière, but slightly more affordable. Lunch by the pool in summer and don't miss the exquisite vegetable tart.

Canto Cigalo Ⓗ
Chemin Canto Cigalo, 13210 St-Rémy. Tel 04 90 92 14 28; fax 04 90 92 24 48. Ⓕ Ⓕ
Small attractive hotel with a garden, off the Cavaillon road.

Impérator-Concorde Ⓗ
Quai de la Fontaine, 30000 Nîmes. Tel 04 66 21 90 30; fax 04 66 67 70 25. Ⓕ Ⓕ Ⓕ
Huge, well-furnished rooms make this the top hotel in Nîmes.

Jules César Ⓗ Ⓡ
Boulevard des Lices, 13200 Arles. Tel 04 90 93 43 20; fax 04 90 93 33 47. Ⓕ Ⓕ
The facade of this former convent conceals flower-filled courtyards and a swimming pool. The Lou Marquès restaurant serves classic food and wines.

Maison Jaune Ⓡ
15 rue Carnot, 13210 St-Rémy. Tel 04 90 92 56 14. Ⓕ Ⓕ
An elegant stone house in the town centre offering serious, deft cooking from local ingredients.

Mas d'Aigret Ⓡ
13520 les Baux. Tel 04 90 54 33 54; fax 04 90 54 41 37. Ⓕ Ⓕ
Delicious Provençal cooking in a most attractive setting.

Hôtel du Musée Ⓗ
11 rue du Grand Prieuré, 13200 Arles. Tel 04 90 93 88 88; fax 04 90 49 98 15. Ⓕ
Lovely old townhouse with a flower-filled courtyard.

L'Oustalou Ⓗ
13520 Mausanne. Tel 04 90 54 32 19; fax 04 90 54 45 57. Ⓕ Ⓕ
Small hotel on the main square, overlooking a charming fountain. One of the few budget options near les Baux.

L'Oustau de Baumanière Ⓗ Ⓡ
Val d'Enfer, 13520 les Baux. Tel 04 90 54 33 07; fax 04 90 54 40 46. Ⓕ Ⓕ Ⓕ
Sumptuous rooms in old stone buildings with superb views. Luxurious restaurant; classic yet simple dishes impeccably prepared. Great but pricy wines.

La Regalido Ⓡ
Rue Frédéric Mistral, 13990 Fontvieille. Tel 04 90 54 60 22; fax 04 90 54 64 29. Ⓕ Ⓕ Ⓕ
Different menus, featuring classic dishes, as well as some (including desserts) made with olive oil. Authoritative wine list.

Wines and Wine Villages

Both les Baux and Nîmes are wonderful places to visit and explore and their vineyards and wine estates lie nearby in beautiful tranquil settings.

Les Baux-de-Provence AC
Formerly part of the Coteaux d'Aix-en-Provence AC, les Baux won its own AC for reds and rosés in 1995. Grenache and Syrah are the principal grape varieties. Some estates have already demonstrated the potential for high quality on the limestone slopes of the Alpilles, but there are still many commonplace wines bearing the AC label. Although no longer entitled to the AC because of its unorthodox blends of Cabernet Sauvignon and Syrah, Trévallon is easily the AC's top producer.
Best producers: *Hauvette,* MAS DE LA DAME, MAS DE GOURGONNIER, ROMANIN, DES TERRES BLANCHES, DE TRÉVALLON.

Costières de Nîmes AC
Formerly known as Costières de Gard, the new name was adopted in 1989 to avoid confusion with other Gard wines. The region is an extension of the Rhône Valley, with similar grape varieties, but with a climate moderated by the marine influence of the Camargue.
  The region lacks a definite style, although many of the best wines are Syrah-dominated. Barrique-aging is rare, and most wines display an attractive purity of fruit. Many wines are still dilute and lacklustre, but more and more estates are intent on improving quality. Rosé accounts for 25 per cent of production, and can be delicious.
Best producers: *Beaubois,* DE BELLE-COSTE, *Lamargue,* MAS NEUF, MOURGUES DU GRÈS, *de Nages.*

East of Aix-en-Provence
the landscape is
dominated by the vast
Mont Ste-Victoire,
immortalized by Cézanne
in his paintings. This
limestone range reaches
an altitude of over 1000m
(3300ft) at its peak and on
its southern side there is a
sheer drop to the valley
below, where grape-
growing is the major
agricultural activity.
These vineyards are near
Rousset and qualify for
the Côtes de Provence
AC, a vast wine region
that stretches across much
of Provence with distinct
viticultural zones. The
Mont Ste-Victoire zone
has rocky soils and a
hotter climate than the
coastal zone.
From the village of
Vauvenargues (where
Picasso is buried in the
park of the château where
he once lived) you can
hike up to the top of the
Mont. From here there
are stunning views south
to the Mediterranean.

Sandwiched between forests of umbrella pines, vineyards on the St-Tropez peninsula benefit from cooling breezes from the nearby sea.

Map illustrations: (left) Ch. Simone in the Palette AC; (right) the Maison des Vins at les Arcs.

Inland Provence

The Provençal hinterland is strewn with vines over an immense area, covered by a number of different appellations. For many years the Côtes de Provence AC was associated with rather bad rosé, and a new generation of dynamic producers is struggling to change the image. Today there are many outstanding estates in the Côtes as well as further west in the Coteaux d'Aix.

The Tour

Begin this tour at St-Tropez, with its beaches, night spots, stars and starlets. If the traffic deters you, stay outside the town on the N98 going west, which brings you to the modern showrooms of the Maîtres Vignerons de la Presqu'Île de St-Tropez, an association of nine estates which have teamed up for blending and marketing purposes. The wide range of products, all fair value within their price band, makes this a good place to stock up on wine and other local produce.

Follow signs to Ste-Maxime, then north to le Muy, where you bear west on the N7; many Côtes de Provence estates

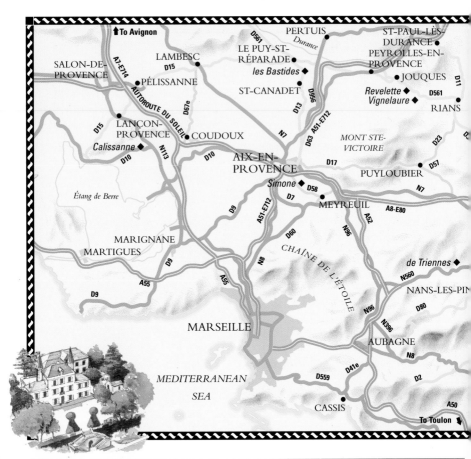

lie alongside this road. At les Arcs you will find the region's Maison des Vins, where the Vinothèque sells 650 different wines from the Côtes de Provence, and an outstanding restaurant, the Bacchus Gourmand, makes a perfect lunch stop.

Just east of the attractive village of les Arcs is Ch. Ste-Roseline, with an abbey dating back to Romanesque times. After the death of the prioress, Roseline de Ville-neuve, in 1330, her corpse was waxed and displayed as an object of veneration. It is still here. The chapel also contains some fine mosaics by Marc Chagall. This estate changed hands in 1994 and Bernard Teillaud, the new owner, has virtually reconstructed the winery and has opened the chapel to visitors. The wines, however, are little changed. The top range is the Tête de Cuvée, which can be impressive but is also very expensive. Considering the AC's poor reputation until a few years ago, it is astonishing how expensive many of the wines are.

Return to the N7 and drive westward. Near Flassans you will find the Commanderie de Peyrassol, another historic property which belonged to the Knights of Malta from the 14th century until the French Revolution. The standard wines here are called Éperon d'Or, and for devotees of new

TOUR SUMMARY

Starting on the coast at St-Tropez, the tour leads inland to les Arcs and Brignoles and then north into the hilly region of Coteaux d'Aix-en-Provence. At le Puy-St-Réparade it turns south to Aix, with an excursion to Salon.

Distance covered 300km (200 miles).

Time needed 2 or 3 days, especially if detours are made to Aix and other Provençal towns.

Terrain For the most part, the route follows good, fast roads which are easy to drive.

Hotels There is a luxurious modern hotel at Rians and several simple but comfortable country inns along the route, but Aix and Salon offer the greatest choice of accommodation.

Restaurants The eastern part of inland Provence is well provided with fine restaurants; except for Aix and Salon, this is not the case further west.

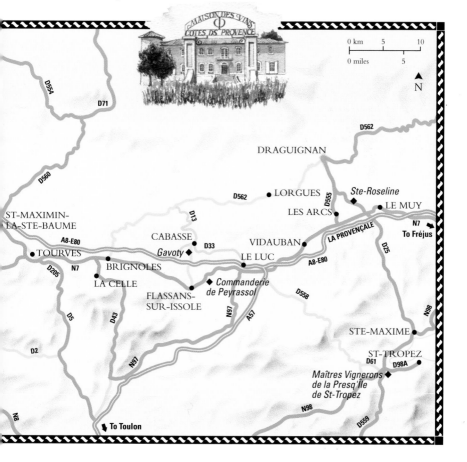

oak there is a considerably more expensive range called Marie-Estelle, and three separate rosé wines.

Just after Flassans, bear right toward Cabasse and you will come to the Domaines Gavoty. Bernard Gavoty, a famous music critic in the 1970s, and his brother owned these two estates near Cabasse. Today they are run by Bernard's niece, who also makes the wines. Unlike the Commanderie, there is little use of new barriques, even for the top Cuvée Clarendon (Gavoty's pen-name). The wines are delicious, well structured, and keep well; the white is one of Provence's best.

Continue along the N7 to Brignoles, where a maze of medieval alleys climbs the hillside. At the top of the town is the 13th-century palace, once the summer residence of the Counts of Provence; now it is a museum full of ancient sarcophagi, dinosaur eggs and wine presses. Further west, at St-Maximin-la-Ste-Baume, is one of the finest Gothic churches in Provence. Work on the basilica began in 1295, after earlier excavations supposedly unearthed the tomb of Mary Magdalene, but the abbey was not completed until 1532. The crypt houses a bizarre gilt reliquary containing, it is said, the skull of Mary Magdalene. Adjoining the basilica is the Couvent Royal, a Gothic monastery with superb flower-filled cloisters, a 13th-century chapel and a spacious chapterhouse. Since 1957 the buildings have served as the town hall and cultural centre.

South-west of Brignoles along the N560 is Domaine de Triennes, an interesting estate owned by two of Burgundy's most celebrated winemakers, Aubert de Villaine and Jacques Seysses. Triennes is technically in the Coteaux Varois, an AC that has been overlooked in Provence, although some estates are making determined efforts to improve their image. It produces a range of varietal and blended wines at very fair prices.

From St-Maximin drive north to Rians, into the Coteaux d'Aix-en-Provence AC. The two estates that lie along the road from Rians to Jouques – Vignelaure and Revelette – produce wines quite different in character from those to the east of St-Maximin. Prolonged winters and cool summer nights produce grapes quite high in acidity, so the wines tend to be tight and vigorous. Vignelaure has always used a high proportion of Cabernet Sauvignon, and the wines keep well. The present owners, the celebrated flying winemaker Hugh Ryman and the former Irish racehorse trainer David O'Brien, who lives at the property, are full of plans for the estate, so it will be interesting to see how it develops.

Revelette is not French-owned either: Peter Fischer is German and trained as a winemaker in California. This is a lovely estate, resembling an open-air lapidary museum studded with peacocks. The white wines, including a

Beautiful Ch. Vignelaure near Rians was a pioneer of quality in Provence in the 1970s and under dynamic new owners is again an estate to watch.

Chardonnay, are unusually sprightly for Provence, and the red Grand Vin, from half Syrah and half Cabernet Sauvignon, is well structured. Fischer uses barriques, but discreetly.

From Jouques carry on to le Puy-St-Réparade, then bear left toward St-Canadet. Before the village you come to Domaine les Bastides, run by Jean Salen and his daughter. Although the vineyards lie at 250–380m (820–1250ft) the grapes ripen magnificently, and the reds are extremely full-flavoured, especially the Cuvée Spéciale, which ages easily for ten years or more, coasting along on richness of fruit rather than high tannin. They also make a delicious rare sweet Provençal *vin cuit*, by reducing the must as if it were a sauce.

Head south toward Aix-en-Provence, and follow signs for the familiar N7. Just south of the city, on the D58 to Meyreuil, is the lovely Ch. Simone, the more important of the two estates that make up the AC of Palette. The vines here, which are on average 60 years old, are planted in a kind of amphitheatre that creates a special mesoclimate for the grapes. The wines are very old-fashioned and not everyone admires them. The red, made partly from varieties, such as Manosquin, which are almost extinct, is robust and earthy, but it's the long-lived white wine that has made Simone's reputation. Also east of Aix is Mont Ste-Victoire, the powerful rock curtain so often painted by Cézanne which rises to more than 1000m (3300ft) above the plain.

Aix-en-Provence is a delightful town: elegant, bourgeois, arty, slightly stuffy. It was founded as a Roman spa in 123BC, and enjoyed a second spell of grandeur from the 12th to the 18th centuries as the capital of Provence. The old town is run through like a sword by Cours Mirabeau, a handsome boulevard shaded by mature plane trees. It is lined on one side with cafés and on the other by splendid town mansions now converted into banks and offices; other fine old mansions house interesting museums.

This tour comes to a natural conclusion at Aix, but the Coteaux d'Aix continues westward for some distance, and there is an exceptionally fine estate, Ch. Calissanne, at Lançon, just south of Salon. It is worth spending the night in Aix and visiting the estate, where archaeological finds suggest that wine was made during Roman times, the following morning. The reds here are made from top varieties such as Cabernet, Syrah and Mourvèdre and Clos Victoire and Cuvée Prestige are outstanding, long-lived wines.

Salon-de-Provence is best known as the home of the Renaissance seer Nostradamus, whose house is close to the clock tower that provides one of the entrances into the old town. This is dominated by the Ch. de l'Emperi, which now contains a museum of military history. Salon is also something of a gastronomic centre, with fine hotels and restaurants on the edge of the town.

Ch. Simone is the main estate in the tiny Palette AC just outside Aix-en-Provence. From the terrace of the elegant château there is a stunning view of Mont Ste-Victoire.

Inland Provence Fact File

Hotels in this sprawling region are modest, but it is well supplied with restaurants – the one at the Maison des Vins is outstanding and it is a useful source of information.

Information

Comité Départemental du Tourisme du Var
1 boulevard Foch, 83003 Draguignan. Tel 04 94 50 55 50; fax 04 94 50 55 51.

Office de Tourisme
21 boulevard Gambetta, 83460 les Arcs. Tel 04 94 73 37 30; fax 04 94 47 47 94.

Maison des Vins - Coteaux Varois
Place des Ormeaux, 83170 la Celle. Tel 04 94 69 33 18; fax 04 94 59 04 47.

Markets

Aix-en-Provence – daily
Salon – Wednesday
St-Maximin – Wednesday
St-Tropez (Maîtres Vignerons de la Presqu'Île) – Sunday morning

Festivals and Events

Two of the larger wine festivals are Coudoux's *Fête de St-Vincent* in January and the *Fête des Vins* in Aix-en-Provence in July.

Where to Buy Wine

Maison des Vins
N7, 83460 les Arcs. Tel 04 94 73 33 38; fax 04 94 47 50 37.
Information on Côtes de Provence wines and 650 wines (from 230 producers) on sale (see Bacchus Gourmand right).

Comptoir des Domaines et Châteaux de Provence
RN7, route de Nice, Brignoles. Tel & fax 04 94 69 41 96.
Estate wines from the central Var.

Cave du Felibrige
8 rue Cordeliers, 13100 Aix-en-Provence. Tel 04 42 96 90 62; fax 04 42 96 26 29.
Outstanding selection of the top wines of Provence.

Where to Stay and Eat

Abbaye de Ste-Croix ®
Route du Val-du-Cuech, 13300 Salon-de-Provence. Tel 04 90 56 24 55; fax 04 90 56 31 12.
Ⓕ Ⓕ Ⓕ
Refined cooking by Pascal Morel in a restored monastery. Good but pricy wine list. Formal service.

Auberge Provençale ®
N7, le Canet, 13590 Meyreuil. Tel 04 42 21 06 23. Ⓕ Ⓕ
Long-established, deservedly popular restaurant east of Aix.

Hôtel des Augustins Ⓗ
3 rue de la Masse, 13090 Aix-en-Provence. Tel 04 42 27 28 59; fax 04 42 26 74 87. Ⓕ Ⓕ Ⓕ
This 12th-century convent in the centre of Aix is now a sumptuous hotel and has been renovated recently.

Chez Bruno ®
Route de Vidauban, 83510 Lorgues. Tel 04 94 73 92 19; fax 04 94 73 78 11. Ⓕ Ⓕ Ⓕ
Epic meals from the larger-than-life figure of Clément Bruno. Truffles are the house speciality.

Bacchus Gourmand ®
Maison des Vins, N7, 83460 les Arcs. Tel 04 94 47 48 47; fax 04 94 47 55 13. Ⓕ Ⓕ
Inventive, well-flavoured food in an attractive setting, offering good value. Terrific regional wines. (See Maison des Vins left.)

Le Bois St-Hubert Ⓗ ®
Route de St-Maximin, 83560 Rians. Tel 04 94 80 31 00; fax 04 94 80 55 71. Ⓕ Ⓕ
Sumptuous, modern, peaceful hotel with a pool, terraces and gardens. Restaurant serves over-elaborate cooking and has only a moderate wine list, but it is the only place in the area.

Chez Nous ®
3-5 boulevard Jean Jaurès, 83470 St-Maximin. Tel 04 94 78 02 57; fax 04 94 78 13 04. Ⓕ Ⓕ
Solid cooking but service can be perfunctory. Disappointing wines.

Le Clos de la Violette ®
10 avenue de la Violette, 13090 Aix-en-Provence. Tel 04 42 23 30 71; fax 04 42 21 93 03.
Ⓕ Ⓕ Ⓕ
Elegant restaurant with cooking to match and summer terrace. Slightly disappointing wine list.

Concorde ®
Place Clemenceau, 83550 Vidauban. Tel 04 94 73 01 19.
Ⓕ Ⓕ
Rustic décor, sound regional cooking, favoured by the locals.

Hôtel Esplanade Ⓗ ®
83560 Rians. Tel 04 94 80 31 12. Ⓕ
Friendly welcome at this no-frills hotel and restaurant.

Hôtel France Ⓗ
Avenue Albert 1er, 83470 St-Maximin. Tel 04 94 78 00 14; fax 04 94 59 83 80. Ⓕ Ⓕ
Pleasant, comfortable hotel in the centre of town.

Logis du Guetteur Ⓗ ®
Place du Château, 83460 les Arcs. Tel 04 94 73 30 82; fax 04 94 73 39 95. Ⓕ Ⓕ
Located in a medieval fortress; pool. Imaginative cooking in a delightful setting. Try the pigeon with truffles. Good wine list.

Mas du Soleil ®
38 chemin St-Côme, 13300 Salon-de-Provence. Tel 04 90 56 06 53; fax 04 90 56 21 52. Ⓕ Ⓕ
Generous classic cooking by Francis Robin in an attractive dining room. The wine list has few regional wines.

Nègre Coste Ⓗ
33 cours Mirabeau, 13090 Aix-en-Provence. Tel 04 42 27 74 22; fax 04 42 26 80 93. Ⓕ Ⓕ
Splendid hotel with spacious rooms in the centre of town.

Le Prieuré Ⓗ
Route des Alpes, 13100 Aix-en-Provence. Tel 04 42 21 05 25; fax 04 42 21 60 56. Ⓕ
This former priory on the outskirts of the town enjoys a verdant, almost rural setting.

Wines and Wine Villages

Apart from Palette, the wine regions here are vast, so it is hard to define their character. But standards are rising fast, and there are some splendid wines on offer. Coteaux d'Aix has exceptional potential, as yet insufficiently realized.

Coteaux d'Aix-en-Provence AC Despite the nondescript reputation of the region, the wines are considerably better than their image. Many estates have made huge efforts to improve quality. The regulations are so broad that it is perfectly possible to produce mediocre wines that satisfy all the rules of the AC, but the better producers work within stricter limits.

This is mostly a region for red wines, since there was no tradition of white-wine drinking in this part of Provence. However, some estates have chosen to produce white wines to complete their range, and some of them are good. But this remains a region where the name of the producer counts for more than the AC. The main problem is high yields and consequent dilution.

Best producers: LES BASTIDES, *Beaupré,* CALISSANNE, REVELETTE, VIGNELAURE.

Coteaux Varois AC This is a large area of 1500ha of vineyards dispersed among 28 communes, and the AC was established only in 1993. It is hard to define its personality, since so many grape varieties are permitted: Grenache, Syrah, Mourvèdre, Carignan, Cinsault and Cabernet Sauvignon for reds; and Rolle, Clairette, Grenache Blanc, Ugni and Sémillon for whites. Consumers are understandably attracted by comparatively low prices, and there are undoubted bargains to be found. Many vineyards are within view of the imposing Massif de Ste-Baume, which offers dramatic hiking country south of Nans-les-Pins.

Best producers: *Chaberts, Garbelle, St-Estève,* DE TRIENNES.

In inland Provence, here near le Luc on the Var plain, grapes and olives are the main crops.

Côtes de Provence AC For decades this AC has been dogged by its undesirable reputation as a mass producer of rosés. There are some very good ones made across this vast region, but the wine estates have become more ambitious. Cellars have been filled with barriques as winemakers seek to produce big, structured red wines and oaky whites, all from a broad palette of grape varieties. The results are of variable quality. Although some wines are truly excellent, prices have risen to exorbitant levels – presumably sustained by summer tourists – and better value is often encountered in Languedoc-Roussillon.

Most vineyards are well away from the small towns and villages of the region, but towns such as Brignoles (visit the medieval palace of the Comtes de Provence, now a museum) and St-Maximin (visit the noble Gothic basilica and the adjoining convent buildings) are well worth exploring.

Best producers: *Bernarde,* COMMANDERIE DE PEYRASSOL, *Courtade,* GAVOTY, MAÎTRES VIGNERONS DE LA PRESQU'ÎLE DE ST-TROPEZ, *Minuty,* RICHEAUME, *Rimauresq,* STE-ROSELINE.

Les Arcs The Maison des Vins (see p.38) stands on the busy N7, but it's worth turning off to the north to visit the village itself. Some pretty lanes lead up to the Saracen tower that dominates it. With its excellent hotels and restaurants, not to mention the facilities of the Maison des Vins nearby, it's an excellent base for visiting the Côtes de Provence.

Palette AC Located just outside Aix-en-Provence, this minute AC has only 23ha of vines. The main estate is the renowned Ch. Simone, with Ch. Crémade in its shadow. As an AC it predates Coteaux d'Aix, having been established in 1948. The personality of the wine derives from the mesoclimate and grape varieties. Vineyards, surrounded by woodlands, face north, yet are planted in an amphitheatre that concentrates the heat. The presence of small quantities of rare varieties, such as Castels and Manosquin, also contributes to the somewhat earthy style of the red. The white, mostly from Clairette, is fermented and aged for about 2 years in old casks. Both wines can be aged for a decade or more. Good rosé too.

Best producers: *Crémade,* SIMONE.

When in Cassis, with its many harbourside restaurants and cafés, the local white wine makes an ideal partner for freshly made bouillabaisse, *coastal Provence's famous aromatic fish stew.*

Cassis and Bandol

The towns of Cassis and Bandol, which lie south-east of the enthralling and underrated city of Marseille, are more familiar to most tourists as coastal resorts than as wine regions. But alongside the cliffs of Cassis are terraced vineyards that make a delicious white wine, and similar terraces in the hinterland of Bandol produce a sensationally rich red.

The Tour

Cassis is a jumped-up fishing port, with pleasant public gardens, a small museum, a ruined castle on a promontory and numerous tourists, and it is here that this tour starts. Cassis is best known for its white wine, usually made from varieties such as Clairette and Ugni. It's not very aromatic, but has sufficient body to accompany the rich garlicky seafood dishes you'll eat at local restaurants. The vineyards are in the hills surrounding the village and form an amphitheatre opening on to the sea.

The wine estates are signposted and easy to find. Domaine de la Ferme Blanche lies alongside the Marseille road just above the town. This is an adventurous estate, where the red wine is partially aged in barriques and a small amount of the white is barrel-fermented. Perhaps the best-known estate is the Clos Ste-Magdelaine, a striking Art Deco villa. The wine here is made from the usual Cassis varieties, with a dash of Sauvignon Blanc. Other Cassis estates with fine reputations include the Clos Val Bruyère and Domaine des Quatre Vents.

If Cassis is easy to visit, the same cannot be said for Bandol. The region is so densely contoured that roads twist and turn confusingly, especially those leading to the more remote hillside estates, and signposts sometimes discontinue halfway along the route. But it's worth persevering, since the wines here are wonderful.

Bandol has a history of viticulture going back to the Phoenician occupation 2500 years ago. Today it owes its lustre to the presence of Mourvèdre, a neurotic red grape variety that requires both intense heat and some maritime influence. It doesn't show well when the vines are young, and the grapes need an alcohol level of 13 degrees if they are to deliver their full potential.

Young Mourvèdre is dense and tannic and it can take a few years before it mellows in bottle and develops its characteristic aromas of leather, game and tobacco. The trick to producing Bandol lies in extracting all that the grape can give without also extracting harsh tannins. Some estates still ferment the grapes with their stalks, which often results in wines that remain undrinkable for decades.

TOUR SUMMARY

Although you can start the tour by driving from Marseille to Cassis, Cassis is by far the more attractive place to stay. From Cassis, the route continues to la Ciotat and Bandol, then inland to some charming villages, before returning to the coast at St-Cyr.

Distance covered 90km (56 miles).

Time needed 1 day.

Terrain Inland, the road passes through a landscape of limestone hills and pine forests. The coastal road, particularly the route des Crètes between la Ciotat and Cassis, gives fabulous views of the cliffs and sea.

Hotels There are few hotels outside Cassis and Bandol, so base yourself on the coast to enjoy the pleasures of port and beach as well as touring.

Restaurants Except for the Hostellerie Bérard in la Cadière, the best restaurants are in Cassis or Bandol, but there are several pleasant country inns.

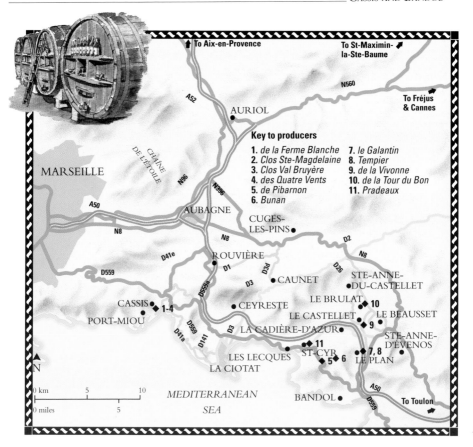

To Aix-en-Provence

To St-Maximin-la-Ste-Baume

N560

To Fréjus & Cannes

AURIOL

Key to producers

1. *de la Ferme Blanche*   7. *le Galantin*
2. *Clos Ste-Magdelaine*   8. *Tempier*
3. *Clos Val Bruyère*   9. *de la Vivonne*
4. *des Quatre Vents*   10. *de la Tour du Bon*
5. *de Pibarnon*   11. *Pradeaux*
6. *Bunan*

MARSEILLE

CHAÎNE DE L'ÉTOILE

AUBAGNE

CUGES-LES-PINS

ROUVIÈRE

CAUNET

STE-ANNE-DU-CASTELLET

CASSIS 1-4

PORT-MIOU

CEYRESTE

LE BRULAT 10

LE CASTELLET 9

LE BEAUSSET

LA CADIÈRE-D'AZUR

STE-ANNE-D'ÉVENOS

11

ST-CYR 7, 8

LES LECQUES

5 6

LE PLAN

LA CIOTAT

N

MEDITERRANEAN SEA

BANDOL

To Toulon

0 km   5   10
0 miles   5

In the 1940s Mourvèdre had almost died out, replaced by varieties such as Carignan and Aramon. Domaine Tempier revived Mourvèdre, and since 1988 red Bandol must contain at least 50 per cent of this variety. Some estates produce wines that are pure Mourvèdre, but grapes of exceptional quality are needed to bring this off. The rosé can be delicious. Mourvèdre gives it some backbone, and Grenache and Cinsault contribute aromatic appeal. Many estates make white Bandol from all sorts of grape varieties, but these are variable in quality and usually overpriced.

To reach Bandol from Cassis, take the D559 road toward la Ciotat. At the main Bandol roundabout head north toward la Cadière, following signs to Ch. de Pibarnon, which can also be approached from the Plan road. De Pibarnon is the creation of Comte Henri de St-Victor, who acquired this beautiful domaine in 1977; it is Bandol's highest estate and the views from here are spectacular. The reds are among Bandol's best and most stylish. Although almost pure Mourvèdre, they never taste harsh and are accessible young but, like all good Bandols, they benefit from bottle-aging. The rosé, too, is extremely elegant.

Descend from de Pibarnon, and follow signs for le Beausset. On the left a road winds up to Domaines Bunan. The

Map illustration: barrel-aging at Ch. de Pibarnon.

Bunan family produces numerous wines, of which the finest is Ch. de la Rouvière, a pure Mourvèdre that is aged for longer than regular Bandol in large casks and a few barriques; it is a very dense wine. Other wines vary in quality, but you can sip before you buy at the well-staffed tasting room.

Continue toward le Beausset, and just before le Plan-du-Castellet, bear right to Domaine du Galantin. This small family operation offers a fine red Bandol at a very reasonable price, and older vintages going back over a decade are still on sale. Some Galantin wines can be a shade tough, but in exceptional vintages their reds are first-rate.

Domaine Tempier is the godfather of Bandol estates as it was its owner, Lucien Peyraud, who died in 1996, who rescued Bandol from obscurity. There are five reds to choose from: the Cuvée Classique (which can be disappointing), the very reliable Cuvée Spéciale, and three single-vineyard wines, Migoua, Tourtine and Cabassaou. Despite Peyraud's passion for Mourvèdre, only Cabassaou is made solely from this grape. These are wonderful wines, richly fruity and densely structured, and they age superbly.

From Tempier continue toward le Beausset, then take a road to the left to le Castellet, which leads shortly to Domaine de la Vivonne. The reds here, which are pure Mourvèdre, receive a touch of barrique-aging and are unfiltered. They are deeply coloured, very dense in their youth, with slight aromas of tar, high in alcohol and definitely need a few years before their wonderful fruit re-emerges.

The hilltop village of le Castellet can be seen beyond Ch. de Pibarnon's vineyards, which enjoy a magnificent location among the pine-clad garrigue high above the valley.

Le Castellet, a manicured medieval village, retains some of the original fortifications and an impressive Romanesque church. Continue to Ste-Anne-du-Castellet and follow signs for la Cadière d'Azur. On the left, a lane leads to Domaine de la Tour du Bon, a tiny estate run by a young and enthusiastic team. The white here is partially fermented in new oak, and the rosé is unusually plump, but it's the red that is particularly impressive, especially the all-Mourvèdre Cuvée St-Ferréol. Despite the use of some new oak, it is packed with fruit and the oakiness is not usually obtrusive.

La Cadière is an attractive village, less self-consciously pretty than le Castellet. One of its attractions is Hostellerie Bérard, the area's finest restaurant. The Bérards are a fount of useful information about the region's food and wines. Continue to St-Cyr, and Ch. Pradeaux, which has been owned by the same family for 250 years. The wines are old-fashioned and almost pure Mourvèdre, and quality has not always been consistent, but Pradeaux at its best is one of Bandol's greatest wines.

From St-Cyr a fast road leads to Bandol itself. The town has a pleasant little port, an impressive casino and ample hotels and restaurants where you can eat wonderful seafood and drink the splendid local wines.

Cassis and Bandol Fact File

Both towns are major tourist centres and are overrun during the summer months. Out of season they are delightful and offer excellent facilities to visitors.

Information

Syndicat d'Initiative
Place Baragon, 13260 Cassis.
Tel 04 42 01 71 17.

Association des Vins de Bandol
23 rue de la République, 83330 le Beausset. Tel 04 94 90 29 59; fax 04 94 98 50 24.

Markets

Bandol, allées Vivien – daily
Cassis – Wednesday and Friday
St-Cyr – Tuesday and Friday

Festivals and Events

Cassis has its *Fête des Vins* in September and Bandol in December. .

Where to Buy Wine

Maison des Vins
Route de Marseille, 13260 Cassis. Tel 04 42 01 15 61; fax 04 42 01 28 01.
Good range of Provençal wines.

Maison des Vins de Bandol/Caveau des Vins
Allées Vivien, 83150 Bandol.
Tel 04 94 29 45 03 & 04 94 29 60 45.
Bandol wines on sale and for tasting.

Exposition Universelle des Vins et Spiritueux
Île de Bendor, 83150 Bandol.
Tel 04 94 29 44 34.
Interesting wine museum.

Where to Stay and Eat

Hostellerie Bérard Ⓗ Ⓡ
Rue Gabriel-Péri, 83740 la Cadière-d'Azur. Tel 04 94 90 11 43; fax 04 94 90 01 94. Ⓕ Ⓕ
Charming old hotel with garden and swimming pool. The family-run restaurant specializes in local produce and has superlative wines.Also 4-day wine courses on offer.

Le Castel Lumière Ⓡ
2 rue Douce, 83330 le Castellet.
Tel 04 94 32 62 20; fax 04 94 32 70 33. Ⓕ Ⓕ
Elegant, but slightly stuffy restaurant with enchanting views, and offering sound local cuisine. The wine list is patchy but fairly inexpensive.

Grand Hôtel des Lecques Ⓗ
Les Lecques, 83270 St-Cyr.
Tel 04 94 26 23 01; fax 04 94 26 10 22. Ⓕ Ⓕ
Sumptuous, tranquil, old-fashioned hotel by the sea.

Île Rousse Ⓗ
17 boulevard Louis Lumière, 83150 Bandol. Tel 04 94 29 33 00; fax 04 94 29 49 49. Ⓕ Ⓕ
Comfortable rooms with fine views. Good swimming pool.

Nino Ⓡ
1 quai Barthélémy, 13260 Cassis.
Tel & fax 04 42 01 74 32. Ⓕ Ⓕ
Bustling seafood restaurant.

La Nonna Ⓡ
La Reppe, 83330 Ste-Anne-d' Évenos. Tel 04 94 90 36 06. Ⓕ Ⓕ
Unpretentious family restaurant, offering delicious food.

Restaurant Presqu'Île Ⓡ
Presqu'Île, 13260 Cassis. Tel 04 42 01 03 77; fax 04 42 01 94 49. Ⓕ Ⓕ Ⓕ
Fashionable and pricy restaurant perched above the cliffs west of town with wonderful views.

Romano Ⓡ
Port de Cassis, 13260 Cassis.
Tel 04 42 01 08 16; fax 04 42 01 37 31. Ⓕ
Smart restaurant with reliable food at sensible prices.

Hôtel Roches Blanches Ⓗ
Route des Calanques, 13260 Cassis. Tel 04 42 01 09 30; fax 04 42 01 94 23. Ⓕ Ⓕ Ⓕ
Luxurious clifftop hotel with swimming pool.

Wines and Wine Villages

In Cassis the vineyards lie above the bustling port and town. In Bandol they are much more dispersed, with many lovely estates in remote spots up in the hills.

Bandol AC Mourvèdre, the main red variety in this scattered AC of 1200ha, needs very hot sites and maritime influence to ripen properly. Tough and tannic when young, the wine mellows to give tremendous aromatic complexity of black fruits, leather and red meat; its resistance to oxidation allows Mourvèdre-based wines to age for decades. Yields are low and chaptalization is forbidden. The wines must be aged for at least 18 months in large casks. Overall, quality is very high, but some estates make wines that stay tough almost indefinitely. *Best producers: Bastide Blanche,* BUNAN, DU GALANTIN, DE PIBARNON, PRADEAUX, *Ste-Anne,* TEMPIER, *Terrebrune,* DE LA TOUR DU BON, DE LA VIVONNE.

Cassis AC It is remarkable that the Cassis vineyards, which gained their AC in 1936, have survived, so great is the pressure on land for new villas. Fortunately regulations now preserve existing forest and vineyard areas. At present there are 168ha of vines, of which 80 per cent are planted with white grapes, mostly Ugni, Clairette, Marsanne, Bourboulenc and Sauvignon Blanc. In a few years the regulations will require at least 60 per cent of Clairette and Marsanne in the blend, which should mean a livelier, more structured wine. The rosés are light and fresh, but the reds sometimes have a tannic edge. *Best producers: Clos Ste-Magdelaine, Clos Val Bruyère,* DE LA FERME BLANCHE, *Mas Calendal, des Quatre Vents.*

The estate of Mas de Daumas Gassac, owned by Aimé Guibert, has played a key role in the transformation of Languedoc wines over the last 20 years and its intensely concentrated red wines have won worldwide acclaim. Nestling in the trees, the beautiful old stone farmhouse, or *mas,* lies in the Hérault hills, surrounded by its vineyards hacked out of the *garrigue*, or scrub, and with the Gorges de l'Hérault beyond. Unbeknown to Guibert when he bought the site, it turned out to have several advantages for growing quality grapes. As well as a unique soil, the orientation is to the cooler north-west and the altitude about 500m (1650ft) above sea level. The Haute Vallée du Gassac benefits from a nocturnal current of cold air, funnelled from the surrounding foothills. The vines flower here about three weeks later than elsewhere in the Languedoc and the harvest is generally later. Guibert has deliberately left as much as possible of the original *garrigue* surrounding each plot of vines to protect the mesoclimate. The Viognier vines in the foreground are used for the white wines which are now almost as acclaimed as the reds.

Hérault and Northern Aude

This tour traverses the Languedoc, which in recent years has become one of Europe's most exciting wine regions. Real attempts are now being made to concentrate wine-making and marketing efforts on the numerous appellations where there is obvious potential for high-quality wines. The approach is twofold. Many growers wish to preserve the typicity of their regions by using local grape varieties and traditions, while others see the future in marketing single-varietal wines as Vins de Pays that compete directly with New World wines. Many Languedoc wine estates pursue both policies simultaneously and the region is in ferment, with wonderful wines emerging from both camps.

The Hérault is almost a monoculture of vines, but has transformed itself in the past decade from an area dominated by unambitious co-operatives into one buzzing with enterprising winemakers. These vineyards are near St-Martin-de-Londres in the Coteaux du Languedoc AC.

Map illustrations: (left) Ch. Villerambert-Julien; (right) the abbey at St-Guilhem-le-Désert.

The Tour

Montpellier is the obvious place to start this tour if you can face the traffic and impenetrable one-way systems. It is a lovely town, rich in old mansions, the Musée Fabre and the vast modern quarter, the Antigone, designed by Catalan architect Ricardo Bofill. Leave the city on the D986 driving

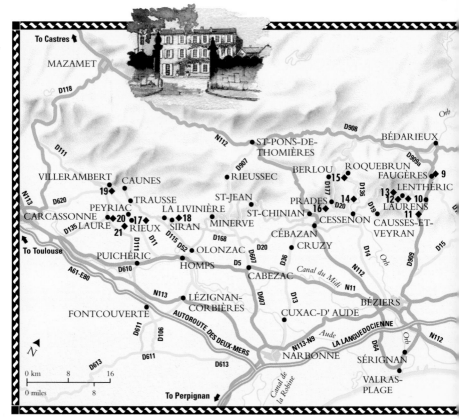

north and following signs for Ganges. At St-Martin-de-Londres, a village with a superb medieval square, turn right to cross Pic St-Loup, one of the new sub-appellations of the Coteaux du Languedoc, a vast AC that groups 156 villages. There are 13 communes in Pic St-Loup, and the dominant varieties are Grenache, Syrah and Mourvèdre. The stony soils are on a bed of limestone and the wines have considerable finesse. This is quite a hilly area, so the wines rarely have the jammy, baked character found in wines from grapes grown on the plain. The best-known estate here is Domaine de l'Hortus, which is well signposted. The location is quite spectacular, with vineyards on facing slopes below two awesome limestone cliffs. The different exposures allow the owner and winemaker Jean Orliac to juggle the different varieties and obtain the best fruit from each. His top wine is the Mourvèdre-dominated Grande Cuvée, but the Cuvée Classique is delicious and accessible young. The neighbouring estate of Mas Bruguière also produces very good wines, and la Roque and de Cazeneuve are other rising stars of Pic St-Loup.

Return to St-Martin and take the D32 to Aniane, where the abbey has a fine Baroque facade. From here the road to Gignac passes the Mas de Daumas Gassac estate. Aimé Guibert threw his family fortune into this remarkable estate

TOUR SUMMARY

A very long tour starting in Montpellier, traversing the Coteaux du Languedoc, Faugères, St-Chinian and Minervois ACs, and ending in the fascinating medieval town of Carcassonne.

Distance covered 400km (250 miles)

Time needed 3 days, but could be prolonged for longer.

Terrain The landscape varies from the coastal plain around Montpellier to the limestone ridge of Pic St-Loup and the gentle southern slopes of the Monts l'Espinouse and the Montagne Noire where they run out into the Aude Valley.

Hotels Montpellier and Carcassonne offer the greatest choice, but there are good hotels in several of the smaller towns.

Restaurants Once again, the greatest choice is in Montpellier and Carcassonne, but there are numerous good restaurants offering local food and wine in country towns and villages.

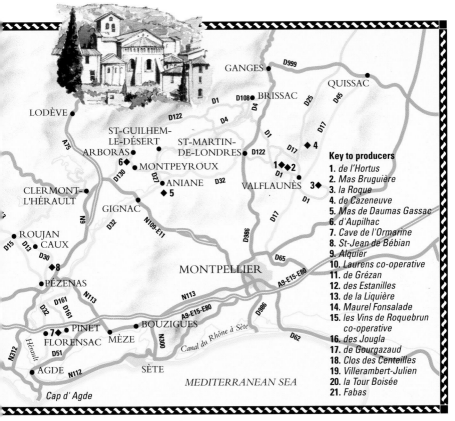

Key to producers
1. de l'Hortus
2. Mas Bruguière
3. la Roque
4. de Cazeneuve
5. Mas de Daumas Gassac
6. d'Aupilhac
7. Cave de l'Ormarine
8. St-Jean de Bébian
9. Alquier
10. Laurens co-operative
11. de Grézan
12. des Estanilles
13. de la Liquière
14. Maurel Fonsalade
15. les Vins de Roquebrun co-operative
16. des Jougla
17. de Gourgazaud
18. Clos des Centeilles
19. Villerambert-Julien
20. la Tour Boisée
21. Fabas

whose soil is crammed with minerals. Although classified as a humble Vin de Pays de l'Hérault, Daumas Gassac has since 1978 been producing Cabernet-dominated wines of astonishing grandeur, richness and longevity. Just as exciting is the exquisitely fragrant white, made from a cocktail of varieties including Chardonnay and Viognier. The estate employs three guides to show visitors around, so despite its exalted reputation no one should feel deterred from visiting.

The winery itself is intriguing: a former flour mill with walls originally built, says Guibert, in Roman times, and subterranean springs which keep the building cool. The glorious Romanesque abbey of St-Guilhem-le-Désert is just to the north and should not be missed.

To the west of Aniane is the unprepossessing village of Montpeyroux, and, on the street leading to Arboras, is Domaine d'Aupilhac's winery. Montpeyroux is another of the Coteaux du Languedoc villages entitled to add its name to the label, and this is its finest estate. After the rich, plump, showy wines of Pic St-Loup, Sylvain Fadat's more austere wine comes as a surprise. His terraced stony vineyards deliver grapes that seem destined for powerful wines. The red is made from equal amounts of Syrah, Carignan, Mourvèdre and Grenache. There is a long maceration period, aging in older barriques, and bottling without filtration. The wine is superb, but demands bottle-aging. More controversial are Fadat's pure Carignan wines, which are an acquired taste.

From Montpeyroux it's a long drive back south from the hills to the flatter coastal lands south-east of Pézenas. The 650ha of vineyards around Pinet are planted with Picpoul, which produces a deliciously bracing white wine. It seems odd that this hot region should produce a wine of such freshness and vigour, but it does, and Picpoul de Pinet is the perfect accompaniment to the local oysters and shellfish. The Pinet co-operative, the Cave de l'Ormarine, accounts for half the production of Picpoul and its wines are good. Some producers leave a little residual sugar in the wine, which not everyone finds desirable, so try to taste before you buy. To enjoy Picpoul in its context, lunch or stay overnight in the coastal villages of Mèze or Bouzigues and drink the wine with local oysters and clams. There are dozens, perhaps hundreds, of shacks and restaurants selling fresh shellfish, so you will be spoiled for choice.

Return to Pézenas, an interesting town with many fine mansions, and take the D30 north toward Caux. This passes the Prieuré de St-Jean de Bébian. Although there is a 12th-century priory here (which for years was owned by the eccentric Alain Roux), it is better known for its superb red wine. The vines — Grenache, Syrah, Mourvèdre — are old and carefully located. Yields were low and fermentations aimed at extracting the maximum. The result was a massive

Fundamental to the quality of Mas de Daumas Gassac's wine is the unusual soil in the vineyards — a deep layer of red, glacial powder interspersed with small stones which offers good drainage and moisture retention along with low organic content.

red, closer in structure to Châteauneuf than to most other Coteaux du Languedoc. In 1994 a French wine journalist, Chantal Lecouty, bought the Prieuré and introduced minor improvements and a high proportion of new oak. The wine today is superb, but expensive.

Turn left on to the D30 and continue north toward Caux and Roujan, where you join the D13, then on past the impressive Ch. de Cassan to the village of Faugères. This is the core of one of the best appellations of the region. In the Faugères AC, as in the neighbouring St-Chinian AC, many vineyards are planted on schist soils; these give specific gamy aromas to the wines, which are made from the usual blend of Carignan, Grenache, Syrah and Mourvèdre.

The cellars of Domaine Gilbert Alquier et Fils are in the village centre. With its array of barriques it looks more like a Burgundian cellar than a Languedoc *cave*. Three red wines are made here, all of outstanding quality, especially the barrique-aged Maison Jaune and the Syrah-dominated les Bastides, which is aged for 14 months in about 50 per cent new oak. Jean-Michel Alquier also makes a superb white wine and sweet Viognier, both barrel-fermented, but there is no AC for the whites.

Laurens lies a few kilometres south of Faugères, and there is an excellent co-operative here, which produces one-third of all the AC wine. Almost all their wines are made by carbonic maceration. The Ch. de Grézan, a sprawling medieval pile that incorporates a restaurant as well as a winery, is also worth visiting. From Laurens drive west to the hamlet of Lenthéric, where you will find the most individualistic of Faugères domaines: Ch. des Estanilles. Michel Luison is a hugely gifted winemaker who happens to find himself based within Faugères. Although his Vin Tradition is a fine classic Faugères, he is better known for his barrique-aged Prestige wine and his glorious Syrah, though Luison won't reveal the precise blend. The rosé, unusually, is barrique-fermented, and his white is a gorgeous blend of Marsanne and Viognier. He calls his top vineyard Clos du Fou because all his neighbours thought he was mad to re-claim a vineyard from such unproductive schist terrain. Luison complains that he is slowing down with age, but his wines have lost none of their flair and brilliance.

If time permits, it's worth driving north a short distance to visit the loquacious Bernard Vidal at Ch. de la Liquière, a traditional domaine producing excellent, reliable wines. Otherwise, drive south-west toward Causses, slipping into the St-Chinian region. Given the similar soils shared by much of Faugères and St-Chinian, it is often difficult to dis-cern any difference between wines from the two ACs.

Pause at the first St-Chinian estate, Ch. Maurel Fonsalade, beautifully located along the D136 in the

Ch. de Grézan is one of the largest wine estates in the Faugères AC and is well organized for visitors. There is also a restaurant built into the castle ramparts which serves wine from the estate.

foothills of the Haut Languedoc. Philippe Maurel runs the domaine, but in the tasting room you may encounter his retired father, whose knowledge of and love for the region are evident. The estate has varied soils, limestone and clay as well as schist, allowing them to produce a range of wines – the best are Cuvée Frédéric and the impressive Fonsalade.

Continue to Causses, and thence north-west to Roquebrun, a fine village sprawled along a hillside. This is the site of an excellent co-operative, the Cave les Vins de Roquebrun. Almost all their wines are made by carbonic maceration, but the preponderance of Syrah and Mourvèdre still gives wines that are well structured and capable of aging. The top wines are aged in new oak. There is also a delicious white wine from barrel-fermented Roussanne and tank-fermented Grenache Blanc. The wines can also be sampled in Roquebrun's restaurants, which are unpretentious but serve good rustic cooking.

From Roquebrun the road follows the river Orb south toward Cessenon, and then west to St-Chinian itself. Just before St-Chinian, turn right to the hamlet of Prades-sur-Vernazobre, where you will find the Domaine des Jougla. Alain Jougla produces three red wines, of which the best is Cuvée Signée, made from old vines planted on schist and partly aged in new oak. All his wines are very reasonably priced and offer exceptional value.

The most direct route from St-Chinian into the Minervois is due west through the hills, but the roads are winding and progress is invariably slow. If time is unlimited, then this is the most scenic route and allows you to visit the former stronghold of Minerve, where in 1210 180 devotees of the Cathar sect died for their faith, a scene that was repeated in many villages of Languedoc and Roussillon. A museum commemorates the Cathars' dogged courage. However, it is much faster to head south via Cébazan and Cruzy to the D5 road linking Béziers and Carcassonne. Head west, then bear right on the D52 toward Olonzac and la Livinière.

Ch. de Gourgazaud, an imposing pink mansion surrounded by an expanse of vineyards and owned by Roger Piquet, lies on the road between la Livinière and Rieux. Gourgazaud is perhaps atypical of the best Minervois estates, offering as it does a wide range of varietal wines as well as classic Minervois blends. Gourgazaud frankly admits that varietal wines are easier to sell. The estate is unashamedly commercial, offering well-made wines at reasonable prices. The top range is the Réserve, aged in new oak, but the standard Cuvée and the Syrah-dominated Cuvée Mathilde offer better value.

Minervois is an enormous region and it is hard, indeed impossible, to define its character, since so many permutations of soil, mesoclimate, grape variety and vinification are

Roquebrun, dominated by its medieval belltower, is an attractive village in the Orb Valley in the southern foothills of the Cévennes.

permitted. The best vineyards face due south toward the sea and the climate tends to be milder than the more extreme conditions encountered in neighbouring Corbières. More attempts are now being made at matching different grapes to the different soil conditions and the best wines will contain as much as 75 per cent of Syrah. Grenache Noir is less prevalent in the blend than in St-Chinian and the rosés are more often dominated by Syrah than Cinsaut.

Siran lies a short distance east of la Livinière, and on its northern fringes, next to a beautifully frescoed Romanesque chapel, is the remarkable Clos des Centeilles. Daniel Domergue and his wife Patricia Boyer have owned vineyards near here since 1975 but bought the Clos only in 1990. The vineyards are of exceptional quality, and the Domergues go to great pains to ensure that only the ripest grapes are harvested, even when, as in 1996, it is tempting to pick fast once the autumn rains have begun. Cinsaut is usually considered suitable only for rosé, but Centeilles produces Cuvée Capitale, a pure Cinsaut red from low-yielding vines, as well as Pinot Noir and more traditional blends. The top wine is Clos Centeilles, from Grenache, Syrah and Mourvèdre grown in an old walled vineyard.

From Siran, where there is a surprisingly good hotel and restaurant for such a tiny village, the Villa d'Eleis, head west to Trausse and Caunes. Caunes is worth a stroll, as it is full of fine Renaissance mansions and has an austere 11th-century abbey. Just off the D620 road to Carcassonne is Ch. Villambert, which is of 16th-century origin. This large estate was split in the 19th century, and the Julien family have managed their half for five generations. Villambert-Julien's wines, both the basic Cuvée Opera and the barrique-aged Trianon, are elegant rather than powerful.

In the Cesse Valley, in the Haut Minervois around the village of Minerve, the vineyards are at a higher altitude and benefit from a slightly cooler climate than elsewhere in the AC.

A narrow road, the D111, cuts south cross-country to Laure, where the dynamic Jean-Louis Poudou runs Domaine la Tour Boisée. He makes good varietal wines, but is prouder of his traditional Minervois, which is extremely good. The best wines are labelled Cuvée Marie-Claude. Poudou also makes delicious whites and wines from botrytized grapes when nature obliges. Just east of Laure is the large Ch. Fabas, which was sold in 1996 to Roland Augustin, a Champagne producer. The best wine here is the Mourvèdre-dominated Cuvée Alexandre. No doubt M. Augustin will stamp his own personality on the estate in years to come.

From Laure it's only a 30-minute drive south-west to Carcassonne. This famous medieval, walled city with its mighty towers is something of a con, since it was largely reconstructed by Viollet-le-Duc in the 19th century, but it caters admirably to tourists and makes an excellent conclusion to a tour of the Minervois.

Hérault and Northern Aude Fact File

Outside the cities of Montpellier and Carcassonne, this is a region of hills and crags, often very beautiful and remote. Accommodation and restaurants tend to be far-flung but are sensibly priced. This is also a popular and rewarding region for camping and hiking.

Information

Comité Départemental du Tourisme de l'Aude
11855 Carcassonne. Tel 04 68 11 66 00; fax 04 68 11 66 01.

Comité Départemental du Tourisme de l'Hérault
Avenue des Moulins, 34034 Montpellier. Tel 04 67 84 71 71; fax 04 67 67 71 77.

Comité Régional du Tourisme Languedoc-Roussillon
20 rue de la République, 34000 Montpellier. Tel 04 67 22 81 00; fax 04 67 58 06 10.

Syndicat des Coteaux du Languedoc
Mas de Saporta, 34970 Lattes. Tel 04 67 06 04 44; fax 04 67 58 05 15.
See also Mas de Saporta right.

Syndicat du Cru Faugères
Ch. de Laurens, 34480 Laurens. Tel 04 67 90 11 12; fax 04 67 90 11 06.
A helpful information office located within the castle.

Syndicat du Cru Minervois
Ch. de Siran, 34210 Siran. Tel 04 68 27 80 00; fax 04 68 27 80 01.

Markets

Carcassonne – Tuesday, Thursday, Saturday
Laure – Sunday
Montpellier – daily in many squares
Pézenas – Saturday

Festivals and Events

Picpoul de Pinet's wine festival is held in early July and St-Chinian has a festival on the first Sunday after July 14.

Where to Buy Wine

Several ACs such as Coteaux du Languedoc and St-Chinian run wine centres that contain retail

The village of St-Guilhem-le-Désert, situated on the edge of its ravine, has changed little since medieval times.

and information outlets, and, in some instances, even restaurants.

Caveau des Vins
Porte de Narbonne, 11000 Carcassonne. Tel 04 68 25 29 38; fax 04 68 11 42 09.

Chai d'Homps
Le Port, 11200 Homps. Tel 04 68 91 18 98; fax 04 68 91 18 99.
Minervois wines and other regional products on sale.

Caves Cairel
5 rue Plan du Parc, 34000 Montpellier. Tel 04 67 92 44 77.
An extensive range of local wines.

Maison des Vins
Avenue de la Promenade, 34260 St-Chinian. Tel 04 67 38 11 69; fax 04 67 38 16 33.
A bright, attractive showcase for St-Chinian wines, as well as an information service.

Mas de Saporta
34970 Lattes. Tel 04 67 92 20 70; fax 04 67 58 05 15.
Just outside Montpellier at the southern interchange of the A9 *autoroute*, this 17th-century *mas*, or farmhouse, is now a major showcase for the wines of Languedoc. As well as many wines on sale, there is a restaurant which offers a wide

choice of reasonably priced menus and wines by the glass.

Where to Stay and Eat

Hôtel d'Alibert Ⓗ
Place de la Mairie, 11160 Caunes. Tel 04 68 78 00 54. Ⓕ
Charming small hotel in an old mansion in the town centre.

Auberge de l'Arbousier ⒽⓇ
Avenue Carcassonne, 11200 Homps. Tel 04 68 91 11 24. Ⓕ
Simple base for visiting the Minervois. The restaurant offers ambitious cooking at bargain prices. Guineafowl is a speciality.

Domaine d'Auriac ⒽⓇ
Route de St-Hilaire, Auriac, 11000 Carcassonne. Tel 04 68 26 72 22; fax 04 68 47 35 54.
ⒻⒻⒻ
This sumptuous, ivy-clad château is set in an ancient park on the southern side of Carcassonne. Generally very expensive but the wines are reasonably priced.

Le Bougainvillea Ⓡ
3 boulevard de l'Esplanade, 34150 Gignac. Tel 04 67 57 50 83; fax 04 67 57 20 13. ⒻⒻ
Sophisticated, perhaps over-complicated, cooking from François Szanto. There is a terrace for summer dining and a good wine list.

Chantovent Ⓡ
34210 Minerve. Tel 04 68 91 14 18; fax 04 68 91 81 99. Ⓕ
Beautifully situated restaurant; plain but satisfying cooking and a fair selection of Minervois wines.

Hôtel de la Cité Ⓗ
Place de l'Église, 11000 Carcassonne. Tel 04 68 25 03 34; fax 04 68 71 50 15. ⒻⒻⒻ
Built into the old city ramparts, this is a small, luxurious hotel with prices to match.

La Côte Bleue ⒽⓇ
34140 Bouzigues. Tel 04 67 78 31 42; fax 04 67 78 35 49. ⒻⒻ
Comfortable motel on the shore of the Midi's oyster capital. Popular and reasonably priced

restaurant specializing in shellfish from the local oyster farms.

Le Grézan ®
Ch. de Grézan, 34480 Laurens. Tel 04 67 90 22 65. ©
A good restaurant built into the ramparts of an impressive château with a terrace for summer dining. The wine list features the estate's own wines.

Le Guilhem ⊞
18 rue Jean Jacques Rousseau, 34000 Montpellier. Tel 04 67 52 90 90; fax 04 67 60 67 67. © ©
Montpellier's most charming hotel, in adjoining mansions. Parking is difficult.

Le Jardin des Sens ®
11 avenue St-Lazare, 34000 Montpellier. Tel 04 67 79 63 38; fax 04 67 72 13 05. © © ©
Not everyone likes the austere décor here, but the cooking by the Pourcel brothers is brilliant and inventive. The wine list is superb.

Léonce ®
2 place de la République, 34510 Florensac. Tel 04 67 77 03 05; fax 04 67 77 88 89. © ©
Jean-Claude Fabre's celebrated restaurant near Pézenas offers rustic cooking executed with finesse. Good local wine list.

Le Logis de Merinville ⊞
Avenue Clemenceau, 11160 Rieux-Minervois. Tel 04 68 78 12 49. ©
Simple, comfortable hotel close to the best Minervois vineyards.

Maison de la Lozère ⊞®
27 rue de l'Aiguillerie, 34000 Montpellier. Tel 04 67 66 36 10; fax 04 67 60 33 22. © ©
A restaurant specializing in local dishes such as *aligot*, thick mashed potatoes flavoured with cheese. Excellent wine list.

Les Mimosas ⊞
Avenue des Orangers, 34460 Roquebrun. Tel & fax 04 67 89 61 36. © ©

The medieval, walled city of Carcassonne has been extensively restored and is well worth visiting.

Handsome town mansion in the heart of St-Chinian, converted by New Zealanders into a luxurious bed and breakfast hotel.

Les Muscardins ®
19 route des Cévennes, 34380 St-Martin-de-Londres. Tel 04 67 55 75 90; fax 04 67 55 70 28. © ©
Excellent and sensibly priced cooking, including game dishes, and regional wines on the edge of the Pic St-Loup.

Hôtel du Parc ⊞
8 rue Achille Bège, 34000 Montpellier. Tel 04 67 41 16 49; fax 04 67 54 10 05. ©
Well-equipped rooms in a 17th-century mansion. A bargain.

Petit Nice ®
34460 Roquebrun. Tel 04 67 89 64 27. ©
An unpretentious restaurant which occasionally serves huge portions of frogs' legs with garlic.

Hostellerie St-Benoit ⊞®
Route St-Guilhem, 34150 Aniane. Tel 04 67 57 71 63; fax 04 67 57 47 10. ©
Modern hotel with a swimming pool on the edge of this delightful village in the depths of the Hérault.

Auberge St-Hubert ®
Avenue des Orangers, 34460 Roquebrun. Tel 04 67 89 50 37. ©

In the heart of the St-Chinian AC, this simple restaurant serves a fine array of inexpensive game dishes in season.

Château St-Martin ®
Montredon, 11000 Carcassonne. Tel 04 68 71 09 53; fax 04 68 25 46 55. © ©
Robust cooking, with well-prepared *cassoulet* and other local dishes. The short wine list concentrates on local wines.

Vieux Moulin ⊞
Chemin de l'Auberge, 34150 Gignac. Tel 04 67 57 57 95; fax 04 67 57 69 19. ©
Pleasant bungalows in a verdant setting near Gignac.

Villa d'Eleis ⊞®
Avenue du Château, 34210 Siran. Tel 04 68 91 55 98; fax 04 68 91 48 34. © ©
Spacious, comfortable rooms in the former château, which is perfectly located for exploring the Minervois. The elegant restaurant offers a luxurious style of cooking, with many local dishes. Very good wine list.

Château de Violet ⊞
Route de Pépieux, 11160 Peyriac-Minervois. Tel 04 68 78 10 42; fax 04 68 78 30 01. © © ©
There's a family atmosphere here: vast bedrooms unaltered in a century, and informal but attentive service. There is also a park and swimming pool.

Wines and Wine Villages

Some of the loveliest countryside in southern France is found in this region. For dramatic landscape it is hard to beat Pic St-Loup, while the remote valleys and hills of Faugères and St-Chinian are tranquil and beautiful. In complete contrast, the vineyards of Pinet are close to the bustling shoreline, where you can eat your fill of local oysters and wash them down with delicious Picpoul wine.

Cabrières (Coteaux du Languedoc AC) This AC, well known for its rosé, comprises about 1000ha around the town of Clermont l'Hérault. The schist soils give its red wines some resemblance to Faugères. An increasing proportion of Syrah in the vineyards is leading to improvements in quality. This is clearly an appellation to watch.
Best producers: Cabrières co-operative, Temple.

Clairette du Languedoc AC Created in 1948, this was the first AC in the Languedoc (and for white wine only from Clairette). The wine comes in varying styles: dry and fortified.
Best producers: Condamine-Bertrand, St-André.

Coteaux du Languedoc AC This immense AC of 50,000ha covers the wines from 156 villages stretching between Narbonne and Nîmes. Once the bargain basement of French wine, with overcropped vineyards planted with dismal grape varieties, it is rapidly being transformed into a source of exceptional fruity wines.

Three sub-regions – Clairette du Languedoc, Faugères and St-Chinian – now have their own ACs, and another 12 wine villages have the right to add their names to the label, sensibly signalling the considerable differences in soil, climate and local tradition that exist across this vast region. Among the better ones for reds are St-Saturnin, Pic St-Loup and la Clape. There are still plenty of

drab and dilute wines here, but at the top level the quality is exciting. For further descriptions see the individual village entries.
Best producers: D'AUPILHAC, Mas Bruguière, MAS JULLIEN, PRIEURÉ DE ST-JEAN DE BÉBIAN.

Coteaux de St-Christol (Coteaux du Languedoc AC) This medium-sized area of 400ha lies between Montpellier and Nîmes. Grenache is the dominant variety, but there are increasing plantings of Syrah and Mourvèdre. Most of these wines are sturdy reds, but there are some full-flavoured rosés, too.
Best producers: la Coste, des Hospitaliers.

Coteaux de Vérargues (Coteaux du Languedoc AC) The slopes of Vérargues produce a medium-bodied red wine, now much enriched by Syrah. The appellation overlaps with that for Muscat de Lunel.
Best producer: Grès-St-Paul.

Faugères AC An AC for red and rosé since 1982, Faugères combines 7 villages with 1780ha of vines in production. The

permitted grape varieties are Carignan, Syrah, Grenache, Mourvèdre and Cinsault, with complex regulations dictating the proportions of each one. In practice, the producers blend as they see fit, with Syrah often dominant. It is the elevation of the vineyards – about 250m (820ft) – and the widespread schist soils that give Faugères its distinction.

The overall quality, from co-operatives as well as private estates, is high, although styles of the wine vary. The carbonic maceration method is used for the simpler wines; those destined for longer life are often vinified traditionally and can be initially austere. Some good white wine is made but it is not entitled to the AC.
Best producers: ALQUIER, DES ESTANILLES, Faugères co-operative, Grézan, Haut Fabregues, LAURENS co-operative, de la Liquière.

Méjanelle (Coteaux du Languedoc AC) Immediately east of Montpellier lies this small zone of 600ha planted on stony, gravelly soils. The wines are mostly sturdy reds that deserve to be better known.
Best producers: Clavel, Flaugergues.

Minervois AC This large region of some 18,000ha sprawls to the north of the Aude river, and the best vineyards lie along the gentle slopes of the Montagne Noire. There are 4 distinct

With its vineyards stretching up into the hills north of Béziers, Faugères, was one of the first Languedoc wine areas to make a name for itself.

sub-regions, each with a different soil and mesoclimate, so it is difficult to generalize about the style of Minervois wine.

The red grapes are the familiar southern French blend of Grenache, Mourvèdre (localized), Syrah, Carignan and Cinsaut. But for its white wines, the Minervois differs from some other southern ACs in using plenty of Roussanne, Marsanne and Bourboulenc. Quality, not surprisingly, is variable, but it has improved considerably over the last decade.

Best producers: CLOS DES CENTEILLES, *Fabas, Gourgazaud, Piccinini,* LA TOUR BOISÉE, VILLERAMBERT-JULIEN.

Pic St-Loup (Coteaux du Languedoc AC)

One of the areas entitled to add its name to the Coteaux du Languedoc AC; 600ha of vines are dispersed between 13 communes. Grenache, Syrah and Mourvèdre must account for 90 per cent of the red wine blend. There are 22 private estates, some producing wines of astonishing quality, in addition to 3 co-operatives. The region is relatively distant from the Mediterranean, and the cool autumn nights give its grapes and wines a remarkable finesse. Pic St-Loup clearly has the potential to produce some of the best wines of southern France.

Best producers: Cazeneuve, DE L'HORTUS, *Lancyre, Mas Bruguière,* LA ROQUE.

Montpeyroux (Coteaux du Languedoc AC)

A ruined château dominates the village of Montpeyroux at the heart of this sub-appellation of 900ha. The wines here are exceptionally robust and in good vintages benefit from aging. The fascinating Romanesque abbey of St-Guilhem-le-Désert is nearby.

Best producers: D'AUPILHAC, *Aiguelière, Font Caude.*

Muscat ACs

Lightly fortified Muscats are made in many corners of Languedoc: at Lunel, Mireval, Frontignan and St-Jean-de-Minervois.

St-Chinian is an up-and-coming AC in the hills north-west of Béziers.

Best producers: la Peyrade (Frontignan), la Cave Rabelais (Mireval), Sigé (St-Jean).

Picpoul de Pinet AC

An AC since 1985, this region of some 650ha south-east of Pézenas produces a delicious, dry white wine that perfectly accompanies the famous local oysters. The Picpoul grape has good acidity, making the wine vibrant and bracing, so much so that some producers leave a little residual sugar in the wine to round it out. There is even a vogue for oak-aging which most admirers of the variety find an abomination. Picpoul is best at its most unadorned. The grapes are invariably machine-picked, so prices are reasonable.

Best producers: Félines, Gaujal, Grangette, Jourdan, DE L'ORMARINE.

St-Chinian AC

The 2000ha of vineyards are dispersed among 20 villages. The vines are mostly planted on south-facing hillsides at up to 300m (1000ft). In the north, the soil is schist, resulting in wines that are hard to distinguish from those of neighbouring Faugères, but to the south there is ample limestone and clay, which gives fruitier, burlier wines. The grapes for red and rosé are Grenache, Cinsaut, Carignan, Mourvèdre and Syrah – with the last two gaining ground. It is difficult to generalize, but most wines are a touch lighter than Faugères wines, although sharing the same flavour spectrum.

Best producers: Coujan, DES JOUGLA, MAUREL FONSALADE, *Rieu-Berlou co-operative,* LES VINS DE ROQUEBRUN.

St-Drézery (Coteaux du Languedoc AC)

This is a little-known region of 420ha north of Montpellier. The soils are alluvial and sandy, so the reds tend to be light and rather rustic.

Best producers: Mas de Carrat, St-Drézery co-operative.

St-Georges d'Orques (Coteaux du Languedoc AC)

A large region of 220ha between Montpellier and Murviel. These are traditional wines of the Languedoc, red and rosé, with considerable amounts of Carignan and Cinsault in the blend.

Best producers: Engarran, Henry, St-Georges co-operative.

St-Saturnin (Coteaux du Languedoc AC)

In rugged landscape west of St-Guilhem-le-Désert, this medium-sized region of 750ha produces some robust red wines. It is best known for its *vin d'une nuit,* which is a light red wine macerated for one night only.

Best producers: St-Saturnin co-operative.

Vin de Pays de l'Hérault

This huge, amorphous region is included here only because an accident of geography has placed within it one of the greatest estates of southern France.

Best producer: MAS DE DAUMAS GASSAC.

These vineyards are near Paziols in the inland, and better, of the two zones of the Fitou AC which are separated by a limestone plateau. The coastal vineyards around the village of Fitou itself generally produce a lighter and softer wine. Half an hour's drive westward up into the wooded hills of the Hautes Corbières is the second zone. Here, clayey-limestone soils have given way to poorer, schistous soils around the rural villages of Tuchan, Cascastel, Paziols and Villeneuve-les-Corbières, where Carignan and Grenache, the principal varieties, can reach their full potential. The vines are lower yielding and the grapes generally ripen a good two weeks later than those grown nearer the coast. The result is a more robust, longer-lived wine which improves with age.

Vines are almost the only crop to thrive in Corbières' poor soils. These vineyards are near Cucugnan in the Hautes Corbières, an arid region producing powerful, full-bodied wines.

Southern Aude

The southern Aude department covers the wine regions of Corbières, Fitou and la Clape. Corbières is mountainous and vineyards tend to be more widespread and more isolated than in the Minervois or other areas of the Languedoc; in all, the Corbières AC covers 11 different zones. For example, around Portel, south of Narbonne and close to the Mediterranean, there is a strange blend of mountain and shore, a different terroir and a mesoclimate that allows Mourvèdre to ripen relatively easily, whereas the Hautes Corbières region around Quéribus has much in common with the more arid parts of Roussillon. Fitou is divided into two very different areas: the inland zone around Tuchan and Villeneuve-les-Corbières, and the coastal zone centred round the village of Fitou itself. La Clape is a sub-region of the Coteaux du Languedoc AC, but since it is so close to Narbonne it seems logical to visit it on this tour.

The Tour

This tour begins in Carcassonne, where the previous tour of the Hérault and the northern Aude ended. Drive east on the fast N113 toward Narbonne, and as you pass through the little town of Barbaira, you will see Ch. Hélène on the right. Unusually for Corbières, where most of the wine estates are located in the hills to the south, this winery, which is not a thing of beauty, is located in a valley. Even more than the Minervois, Corbières is an extremely varied region, with estates dispersed throughout. Here in the north is the Montagne d'Alaric, and Ch. Hélène's vineyards lie along its limestone slopes.

Marie-Hélène Gau, a psychologist, acquired Ch. Hélène in Barbaira in 1977 and has bottled her wines since 1984. In the early 1990s she handed the reins to her daughter, who has made few changes. The wines all bear classical references. The basic range is the unoaked Cuvée Pénélope; Cuvée Ulysse has a higher proportion of Syrah and is aged in older barriques. The top wine is grandly named Cuvée Hélène de Troie and is almost pure Syrah aged in new oak. There's also a white barrel-fermented Hélène de Troie. These may not be the most characteristic Corbières wines, but they are sound, enjoyable and reasonably priced.

Continue on the N113 toward Narbonne until, on the right, you see a sign for Moux. Ch. Manseroble is in the centre of this village. The owner, Guido Jansegers, pursued wine as a hobby in his native Belgium and was acclaimed as the country's best taster. A few years ago, when he reached the age of 50, he decided to make wine rather than write about it, and settled upon this estate in the Montagne

TOUR SUMMARY

From Carcassonne, the tour follows the Aude Valley for a short distance, then wanders southward through many small villages as far as Rivesaltes. From here it returns north to the region of la Clape, just outside Narbonne.

Distance covered 310km (206 miles)

Time needed 2–3 days

Terrain Inland this is rugged mountain scenery for the most part, with twisting and often narrow roads. Along the coast there is some flat coastal scenery and a fast motorway.

Hotels There is little accommodation in the southern Aude except in larger towns such as Narbonne and Lézignan-Corbières.

Restaurants There are two outstanding country restaurants, one at Fontjoncouse and one at at Durban-Corbières. Otherwise, most of the better restaurants are in Narbonne.

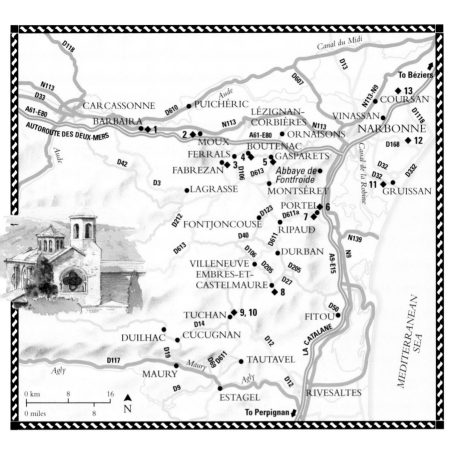

d'Alaric. Possibly aided by Jansegers' excellent contacts throughout the wine world, the Mansenoble wine has been a great success. Many estates in Corbières use carbonic maceration, but not Mansenoble. Jansegers also keeps his yields low, so the wines, especially the splendid Réserve red, are very concentrated.

From Moux follow the signs for Fabrezan, where there is a co-operative named after the poet Charles Cros, who was born here. There are many co-operatives in Corbières and this is one of the more dynamic ones. All its grapes, except for Grenache, are vinified by carbonic maceration, but the wines are not excessively soft or plump. The basic range, labelled Arpège, is a touch rustic but very good value. The Prieuré de la Bernède is Syrah-dominated but unoaked, so the fruit comes shining through. The best wine, called Delicatesse, is mostly Syrah, but it is aged for 15 months in barriques to give it suppleness and concentration.

From Fabrezan head east toward Ferrals-les-Corbières, then follow signs for Boutenac; the D161 traverses some fairly wild countryside covered with aromatic shrubs known as *garrigue*. Domaine de Fontsainte is located in Boutenac; its wine is good but the proprietor is crusty and not very welcoming. Continue east to the hamlet of Gasparets,

Map illustration: the Cistercian abbey of Fontfroide.

Key to producers
1. *Hélène*
2. *Mansenoble*
3. *Charles Cros co-operative*
4. *de Fontsainte*
5. *la Voulte-Gasparets*
6. *de Lastours*
7. *Haut-Gléon*
8. *Castelmaure co-operative*
9. *de Nouvelles*
10. *Producteurs du Mont Tauch*
11. *de Capitoul*
12. *de l'Hospitalet*
13. *Pech-Céleyran*

where you will find Ch. la Voulte-Gasparets in the heart of the village. Patrick Reverdy is the sixth generation of his family to make wine here, and it is truly excellent. Despite the use of carbonic maceration, even his basic wine, the Cuvée Réservée, has good structure and ages well and the barrique-aged Cuvée Romain Pauc is exceptionally fine, although expensive for Corbières.

From Gasparets continue south as far as the D613. It's a bit of a detour, but it is worth driving toward Narbonne on this road until you see signs on the right for the abbey of Fontfroide. Don't miss the opportunity of visiting this beautifully preserved 12th-century Cistercian abbey. You may wish to stay the night in Narbonne, since this part of the Corbières region is poorly supplied with hotels.

Otherwise, you can reach Portel on country roads, travelling west from Fontfroide toward Monséret on the D423, then south to Ripaud and east to Portel on the D611. From Narbonne, simply take the A9-E15 *autoroute* south to the Portel exit. Portel is an uninteresting little village, but just to the west of it is the astonishing Ch. de Lastours.

This large estate performs many functions. It is primarily a home for the mentally handicapped, who tend the vineyards; it is also a four-wheel-drive race track, and some visitors have found themselves treated to an alarming jeep ride around the almost perpendicular hills that embrace the vineyards. There is also a restaurant at the château. Despite a high proportion of the often dour Carignan grapes in the blends, the wines of Lastours are consistently excellent and inexpensive. Its neighbour, Haut-Gléon, is another of the top estates in Corbières.

The elegant 13th-century cloisters with their slender marble columns are just one of the sights at the abbey of Fontfroide, tucked away in a deep valley near Narbonne.

If it is nearly lunchtime, continue westward up the D123, a twisting mountain road, to the tiny village of Fontjoncouse, where you will find the Vieux Puits restaurant; the chef, Gilles Goujon, is considered the best in the Corbières. Then return to the D611 and continue south to Durban-Corbières, where there is a ruined castle. On the hillside above the village is the region's other outstanding restaurant, David Moreno's le Moulin.

As you travel southward on the D611, you cross one of the loveliest parts of the Corbières, with woodland and pasture as well as vineyards. After Villeneuve-les-Corbières, bear left to Embres-et-Castelmaure. The co-operative here looks shabby, but the wines are good and cheap. Except for Grenache, all varieties are made by carbonic maceration. The best grapes come from schist and limestone soils in the area and the wines are given some aging in barriques.

Carry on to Tuchan on the D611. You are now in Fitou, which is essentially a sub-region of Corbières with its own AC. Production in Fitou is dominated by the co-operatives, but their wines are often superior to those from the handful of private estates, such as the well-known but sometimes disappointing Ch. de Nouvelles at Tuchan. The Producteurs du Mont Tauch co-operative at Tuchan is excellent, offering a wide range of single-vineyard wines as well as blends at various quality and price levels.

You are quite close here to some of the most dramatic countryside of the Languedoc, studded with ruinous Cathar castles. The Cathars were a Christian sect, which flourished here between the 11th and 13th centuries, until it was ruthlessly suppressed by Simon de Montfort. The 11th-century fortress at Quéribus lies just south of Cucugnan, and the Ch. de Peyrepetuse is near Duilhac. These old villages and castles, so rich in history, are well worth visiting, but they will take you further and further away from Narbonne. Closer to your route, you can visit the Cathar Ch. d'Aguilar in Tuchan, then head south-east to Rivesaltes, where the A9-E15 motorway leads back to Narbonne.

There is no need to go into Narbonne itself to visit la Clape. Instead, take the *autoroute* Exit 37 for Gruissan and Narbonne-Plage and then follow signs to the former. The Montagne de la Clape looms up in the distance out of the plain, a surprisingly inhospitable landscape given its proximity both to the shore and to Narbonne. On the right you will find Ch. de Capitoul. Although less well known than some other estates in the region, the wines here are first-rate. Both red wines are particularly good, and there is stunning but very expensive Viognier, aged mostly in new oak.

Continue along the D332, following the signs to Narbonne-Plage, a popular, modern, summer beach resort, then take the D168 toward Narbonne, crossing the wild heart of la Clape, covered with pine forests and vineyards. You can't miss the new vineyards of Domaine de l'Hospitalet on the left. This extraordinary estate is more than a winery: it incorporates 16 museums on themes such as telephones, honey and old cars, two restaurants, a hotel and various boutiques. The cellars are large enough to contain 3600 barrels, but the quality of the wines is patchy and they are not cheap, so taste before buying.

Continue across the Montagne, bear right off the D168 to Vinassan and on to Coursan. On the right is Ch. Céleyran, the seat of the Toulouse-Lautrec family, and opposite is Ch. Pech-Céleyran, owned by an equally illustrious family, the St-Exupérys. Like the other estates of la Clape, it produces both AC wines and Vins de Pays, including two Chardonnays, a Viognier, and – a rarity in la Clape – a Pinot Noir.

From here it is only a short drive back to Narbonne. The city's old centre, with its cathedral and immense archbishop's palace, is most attractive. Narbonne is traversed by the Canal de la Robine, whose banks are lined with food and newspaper stalls and markets.

On its hilltop site the impressive castle of Aguilar stands high above the Fitou vineyards near Tuchan.

Southern Aude Fact File

It is easy to lose oneself in the often wild landscape of the Corbières but fortunately, there are many attractive places to stay and eat. Good free guides to the vineyards are available.

Information

Comité Départementale du Tourisme de l'Aude
See p.52.

Syndicat de l'AOC Corbières
Maison des Terroirs, N113, 11200 Lézignan-Corbières. Tel 04 68 27 73 00; fax 04 68 27 31 66.
Produces excellent touring guides to the Corbières vineyards.

Syndicat du Cru Fitou
Maison des Terroirs, N113, 11200 Lézignan-Corbières. Tel 04 68 27 73 09; fax 04 68 27 31 66.

Markets

Lézignan – Wednesday
Narbonne – daily in les Halles, outdoors on Thursday

Festivals and Events

Tuchan holds a wine festival in late July, Fitou in August and Lézignan at the end of October.

Where to Buy Wine

Palais du Vin
Domaine St-Créscent, route de Perpignan, 11100 Narbonne. Tel 04 68 41 47 20.
Good regional selection, as well as wines from the rest of France.

Where to Stay and Eat

L'Alsace ®
2 avenue Pierre Sémard, 11100 Narbonne. Tel 04 68 65 10 24; fax 04 68 90 79 45. Ⓕ
Very comfortable, family-run restaurant specializing in shellfish rather than dishes from Alsace.

La Balade Gourmande ®
Chemin du Moulin à Vent, N113, 11200 Lézignan-Corbières. Tel 04 68 27 22 18. Ⓕ
Good local food, including fish. *Foie gras* is also a speciality here.

La Cave d'Agnès ®
11510 Fitou. Tel 04 68 45 75 91. Ⓕ
Home cooking and grills in an old wine cellar. Local wine list.

Claude Giraud ®
Domaine de St-Créscent-le-Vieil, 11100 Narbonne. Tel 04 68 45 28 50; fax 04 68 45 28 78. ⒻⒻ
Giraud, Narbonne's leading restaurateur, is now located in this old vaulted building. Highly accomplished cooking and good local wines.

Le Clos des Souquets ®
Avenue de Lagrasse, 11200 Fabrezan. Tel 04 68 43 52 61. Ⓕ
Sound unpretentious cooking and an excellent wine list.

Auberge de Cucugnan ®
2 place Fontaine, 11350 Cucugnan. Tel 04 68 45 40 84; fax 04 68 45 01 52. Ⓕ
A well-known restaurant in the Hautes Corbières, specializing in dishes such as wild boar.

Grand Hôtel du Languedoc Ⓗ
22 boulevard Gambetta, 11100 Narbonne. Tel 04 68 65 14 74; fax 04 68 65 81 48. Ⓕ
This attractive old house is now a hotel with comfortable bedrooms at sensible prices.

Grange des Mizels ®
Domaine de l'Hospitalet, route de Narbonne-Plage, 11100 Narbonne. Tel 04 68 45 28 50; fax 04 68 45 28 78. ⒻⒻ
Located in a 16th-century barn at the ever-expanding de l'Hospitalet complex, with menus inclusive of wine from the estate. (See Auberge des Vignes.)

Le Moulin ®
11360 Durban-Corbières. Tel 04 68 45 81 03; fax 04 68 45 83 31. ⒻⒻ
Since it opened in 1991, this restaurant on a remote Corbières hilltop has won rapid acclaim for its young chef, David Moreno.

Le Petit Comptoir ®
4 boulevard Maréchal Joffre, 11100 Narbonne. Tel 04 68 42 30 35. Ⓕ

Cosy little bar and restaurant, serving hearty local food, including good desserts. There is a short but well-chosen list of local wines.

La Résidence Ⓗ
6 rue du 1er Mai, 11100 Narbonne. Tel 04 68 32 19 41; fax 04 68 65 51 82. ⒻⒻ
Comfortable quiet hotel in the heart of the city, with helpful management.

Hôtel Tassigny Ⓗ
Place de Lattre de Tassigny, 11200 Lézignan-Corbières. Tel 04 68 27 11 51; fax 04 68 27 67 31. Ⓕ
One of the few acceptable inexpensive hotels in the Corbières region.

Relais du Val d'Orbieu Ⓗ®
D24, 11200 Ornaisons. Tel 04 68 27 10 27; fax 04 68 27 52 44. ⒻⒻ
A former mill converted into a small, comfortable resort hotel with peaceful gardens, tennis courts and swimming pool. Excellent restaurant.

Auberge du Vieux Puits ®
11360 Fontjoncouse. Tel 04 68 44 07 37; fax 04 68 44 08 31. ⒻⒻ
Brilliant and generous cooking from Gilles Goujon, using superb local ingredients. The *sommelier* is outstanding.

L'Auberge du Vigneron Ⓗ®
2 rue Achille Mir, 11350 Cucugnan. Tel 04 68 45 03 00; fax 04 68 45 03 08. Ⓕ
Unpretentious hotel in a remote but popular village in the Hautes Corbières. Attractive dining room, where robust dishes such as *canard farci* are served.

Auberge des Vignes Ⓗ
Domaine de l'Hospitalet, route de Narbonne-Plage, 11100 Narbonne. Tel 04 68 45 28 50; fax 04 68 45 28 78. ⒻⒻ
The large de l'Hospitalet complex (see Grange des Mizels and p.61) includes a comfortable hotel.

Wines and Wine Villages

The Corbières region boasts numerous Cathar castles, many of which can be visited, and remote countryside. La Clape is immediately inland from the spacious beaches of the Narbonne coast, so you can easily combine sea bathing with wine-tasting.

La Clape (Coteaux du Languedoc AC)   This is one of the best Coteaux du Languedoc sub-regions with about 1000ha of vines. Once an island, the la Clape mountain is mostly limestone, but the region also benefits from its proximity to the sea, abundant sunshine and a frequent drying wind that keeps the grapes healthy.

Red, white and rosé wines are produced, and the white is supposed to be dominated by Bourboulenc. Most estates also produce a range of varietal Vins de Pays, and some attractive Chardonnay and Viognier wines are now emerging. As for the reds, Grenache is used less frequently here than in other parts of the Coteaux du Languedoc, and, as elsewhere, Syrah is becoming increasingly popular. In style, the wines tend to be medium-bodied, elegant, and designed for medium-term drinking. There is little of the rusticity often encountered in nearby Corbières.
Best producers: DE CAPITOUL, DE L'HOSPITALET, PECH-CÉLEYRAN, Pech Redon, Rouquette-sur-Mer.

Corbières AC   A huge region, with some 14,000ha producing mostly red wine. It is divided into 11 sub-regions, each with a marked character of its own, owing to varying soil structures and mesoclimates. Until the early 1980s the wine had a rustic character because of the high proportion of Carignan, but the introduction of better varieties, such as Syrah and Mourvèdre, has improved the quality. Technically progressive co-operatives, as well as a growing number of quality-conscious private estates, have transformed the region, which is only now beginning to realize its potential. The widespread use of carbonic maceration has toned down the rusticity of much of the wine, but some top estates are returning to traditional vinification in order to capture the typicity of individual terroirs. With a few exceptions, the white wines lack character.

There is plenty to see in the region other than wine estates. There are small towns, such as Durban and Lézignan, but the main attractions are churches and castles. The cathedral and ecclesiastical palace at Narbonne and the Cistercian abbey of Fontfroide, just west of Narbonne, are deeply impressive, and there are splendid romantic Cathar castles at Durban, Villerouge, Quéribus, Durfort and Peyrepetuse. The powerful keep at Arques is particularly well preserved.
Best producers: CASTELMAURE co-operative, CHARLES CROS, Fontsainte, Haut-Gléon, HÉLÈNE, DE LASTOURS, MANSENOBLE, ST-AURIOL, Trillol, LA VOULTE-GASPARETS.

Fitou AC   Tucked into the Corbières region, this is the oldest Languedoc AC, dating from 1948. It is divided into 2 distinct zones: the inland one around Tuchan, which usually produces the better wine, and the coastal one around Fitou itself. The inland zone has Syrah but no Mourvèdre; near Fitou it is the other way round. It is not always easy to distinguish Fitou wine from Corbières but it tends to be slightly more robust. Carignan is the main grape, since the wine must contain 40 per cent of the variety. The wine is aged for at least 18 months before bottling. Co-operatives have taken the lead in terms of quality and quantity, and now make some impressive oaked wines available. Prices remain modest. Inland Fitou is a varied and beautifully hilly landscape of woods as well as vineyards.
Best producers: Cave de Villeneuve-les-Corbières, MONT TAUCH, Nouvelles.

Quatourze (Coteaux du Languedoc AC)   This little-known 200-ha sub-region is gradually being absorbed into the Narbonne suburbs. The red wines can be quite austere, but there are some attractive rosés. Carignan is the main grape variety.
Best producers: Cave St-Charles du Quatourze, Notre Dame.

The village of Paziols is in the heartland of the Fitou AC, in the rugged hills of the Hautes Corbières.

Roussillon

On the border between Languedoc and Roussillon, and sheltered by a ridge of high limestone cliffs, the Tautavel vineyards produce Côtes du Roussillon-Villages as well as the local fortified wine, Rivesaltes.

Although Roussillon borders the Languedoc, its wines have a very different character. This is Catalan territory, tucked against the foothills of the Pyrenees, and the Catalan language is still widely spoken.

The Tour

Perpignan is a sprawling town living off its fruit and vegetable markets and tourism. It is dominated by the fortress of the Kings of Majorca, who were the rulers here in the 13th century. The old town, much of which is a pedestrian quarter, is pleasant, but there are only a few older buildings of great interest, and the cathedral is overshadowed by the splendid secularized church of St-Dominique. The gorgeous 14th-century Gothic palace, the Loge de Mer, now houses a branch of a fast-food chain. But there are attractive walks along the café-lined river Basse, which borders the old town. Perpignan is an excellent base for visiting Prades (where the celebrated cellist Pablo Casals created a great music festival), Céret with its modern art museum, the fine Romanesque priory at Serrabone, and other historic sites.

Leave Perpignan on the A9-E15, heading north toward Rivesaltes. The town has given its name to two fortified wines, or Vins Doux Naturels, which are some of France's best. These wines are made by arresting fermentation with spirit; the unfermented grape sugar remains in the wine, giving it its residual sweetness, and aging in large casks gives the wine its aromatic complexity. The leading producer here is Domaine Cazes, located in the village centre. This huge estate is run by two brothers, who combine innovation with the highest standards, and their fortified wines are all superb and underpriced for the quality. There are also various ranges of Vins de Pays, some using Cabernet Sauvignon and Merlot, which are not traditional Roussillon vines but give very good grapes. The Côtes du Roussillon-Villages, a blend of Grenache, Syrah and Mourvèdre, is usually the best red, although a strong rival has emerged in the form of Le Crédo, a Bordeaux blend aged in new oak.

From Rivesaltes take the D117 west to Espira-de-l'Agly, where another fine estate, Piquemal, is also tucked away in the village centre. From here, head south a short distance to Baixas, where the co-operative is the largest and probably the best in Roussillon. In the centre of Baixas is the Ch. les Pins, which is leased by the co-operative from the municipality and gives its name to their best wines. There is also a fine range of fortified wines.

From Baixas a narrow road, the D18, leads into the hills to the west. At the hamlet of Calce you will find Domaine

TOUR SUMMARY

Based around Perpignan, the tour begins by heading north to visit estates around Rivesaltes. It then continues south of Perpignan to visit estates within the famous coastal wine regions of Collioure and Banyuls.

Distance covered 180km (110 miles).

Time needed 2 days.

Terrain The distances covered are not great but some of the roads in the first part of the tour are fairly mountainous and winding.

Hotels Except for Perpignan and the coastal villages, the region is not very well served by places to stay.

Restaurants There are several good restaurants along the coast serving local specialities. Roussillon's top chef, Didier Banyols, is based inland at les Feuillants in Céret.

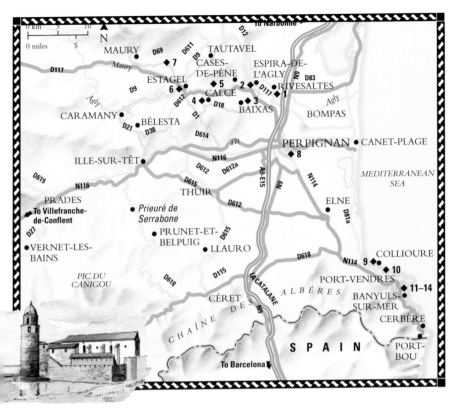

Map illustration: the fortified church at Collioure.

Gauby. Gérard Gauby, built like a rugby player, has trans-formed a traditional, small family estate into one of the leading estates of Roussillon. Like many producers, he is not too worried about whether or not his wines obey the AC rules. If they do, fine; if not, they are labelled Vin de Pays. His Côtes du Roussillon is usually a dense, smoky wine, and his Villages red is made from older vines and aged for longer in barriques. His whites are remarkable: ultra-ripe Viognier aged in partially new oak, and Grenache Blanc, also aged in barriques, which shows how good this maligned variety can be if yields are kept low.

Return to Baixas and Espira, then pick up the D117 to Estagel. Continue westward to Cases-de-Pène and turn off to the right to visit Ch. de Jau. This lovely domaine is more than a wine estate. Art exhibitions are held here, and the restaurant offers simple set menus with a range of Jau wines by the glass. Jau's best wines come from Clos de Paulilles, which is in Collioure and produces a delicious Collioure, rosé as well as red.

Return to the main road and continue westward. At Estagel you can visit the Domaines des Schistes, which pro-duces robust reds from very arid vineyards. Just after Estagel, the D611, then the D9, wind northward to the interesting little town of Tautavel, where there is a good museum of prehistory. Back on the D117, almost at once take the D69

Key to producers

1. Cazes
2. Piquemal
3. Baixas co-operative
4. Gauby
5. de Jau
6. des Schistes
7. Mas Amiel
8. Sarda-Malet
9. la Tour Vieille
10. Clos de Paulilles
11. Cellier des Templiers
12. du Mas Blanc
13. de la Rectorie
14. l'Étoile co-operative

in the direction of Maury, and just after the turning you will come to Mas Amiel.

Mas Amiel is the leading estate within the Maury appellation. Quality here has always been first-rate, but these rich, long-lived fortified wines were neglected until a few years ago, when *sommeliers* realized how well the wines match chocolate-based desserts. Now Mas Amiel has become fashionable. It is the vintage style that is in demand, but many admirers of these wines prefer the wines that are aged for years, even decades, in large oak casks, gaining in concentration and subtlety as they slowly evaporate. The wines also spend a year or so in *bonbonnes,* large glass jars that remain outside for 12 months or so, with the purpose of giving the wines the distinctive oxidative flavour (often resembling that of dry sherry) known as *rancio.*

The vineyards here are particularly parched, and the same is true of those around Maury itself, where the co-operative is based. The village is only a few miles south of the spectacularly sited Ch. de Quéribus, the last Cathar castle to be captured in 1255, and some of the more picturesque corners of the Corbières can be visited from here. The ruins of Ch. Peyrepetuse can be seen across the valley.

Return to Perpignan. There's an interesting estate on the edge of the city, but it's quite hard to find. This is Domaine Sarda-Malet, located along a lane that starts close to the prison and the *autoroute* entrance at Perpignan Sud. Unlike many Côtes du Roussillon estates, Sarda-Malet is sparing in its use of carbonic maceration. There are a number of wines, including the Terroir Mailloles, which is half Syrah-half Mourvèdre and aged for eight months in new oak. The Rivesaltes is exceptionally good here, and the owner, Suzy Malet, has created a delicious but expensive late-picked Malvoisie wine called l'Abandon.

The N114 leads south from Perpignan to the coastal resorts of Collioure and Banyuls, which are very close to the Spanish border. These are charming ports, hemmed in by mountains extensively planted with vines. The soil here is very thin, yields are low, and a few decades ago many of the more remote vineyards were being abandoned. Today, quality-conscious winemakers are bringing them back into production, since everyone acknowledges that this corner of Roussillon produces exceptional wine: both the powerful reds and rosés, often with a large proprtion of Mourvèdre, sold as Collioure, and the fortified wines made from Grenache and sold as Banyuls.

In Collioure, down by the port and not far from the 14th-century castle, is the tasting room for Domaine la Tour Vieille. This estate produces a full-bodied white from Grenache Gris, Collioure rosé, and two reds, of which the more characterful is Cuvée Puig Oriol from Grenache and

The Mas Amiel estate just outside Maury still uses the traditional method of aging the wines. These are left outside in large glass jars, or bonbonnes, for a period of 12 months so that the wine is exposed to the full range of seasonal temperatures.

Syrah. There's a fascinating wine called Cap de Creus, which is essentially a Banyuls that has been fermented close to dryness. This is a rich and alcoholic wine with a *rancio* flavour, not unlike a Vin Jaune from the Jura. Thirty years ago this was the traditional wine of the region, and it is a fine complement to Collioure's gastronomic speciality of fresh anchovies.

In Port-Vendres, the next village along the coast you will pass Clos de Paulilles, and you may well have tasted the wines at Ch. de Jau, since the two estates share a common owner. In Banyuls itself there are a number of estates, and all the wineries, except for the large co-operative, the Cellier des Templiers, are located behind the port. The Templiers' cellars and tasting room lie just west of Banyuls and are clearly signposted. The wide range available here makes this a good place to become acquainted with the different local wines. The Templiers produce 85 per cent of all Collioure, and many single-domaine wines within that appellation. There are many styles of Banyuls on offer, from youthful red and white Banyuls to purple, vintage-type wines (known as Rimage) and traditional Banyuls, aged for 15 years or more in large casks. Vintage Banyuls, although less tannic than vintage port, needs to be bottle-aged; traditional Banyuls is ready to drink when purchased.

Within Banyuls itself the best-known estate is the Domaine du Mas Blanc, whose proprietor, Dr André Parcé helped to restore the wine's reputation after World War Two and who virtually created the Collioure appellation. Dr Parcé is now retired, and the wines are less consistent than they used to be. The Parcé brothers, distant cousins of the doctor, run an excellent estate called la Rectorie. Their wines are greatly in demand and quite expensive. There are several Collioures, all dominated by Grenache; le Seris and Coume Pascole are barrique-aged wines and need time to develop. There's a delicious white called l'Argile, and different Banyuls, of which Cuvée Léon Parcé is the best known and most reliable.

You will also find Banyuls' other co-operative, l'Étoile, in the village. This produces excellent traditional Banyuls, with different bottlings reflecting the age of the wine, the grape blend and the level of sweetness. In many instances they reflect individual tastes rather than quality levels. In addition, there are Rimage wines and some Collioures of variable quality.

These coastal villages have good restaurants, where it is possible to drink the wines with local specialities, such as anchovies with red peppers, and a range of Catalan dishes. Most restaurants serve Banyuls by the glass. High summer is not the best time to visit the ports, since they are inundated by mostly French tourists.

Port-Vendres is an important centre for anchovy fishing and its vineyards are included in the Collioure and Banyuls ACs. This stretch of beautiful rocky coastline, with its brilliant dazzling light, is called the Côte Vermeille and has inspired many artists.

Roussillon Fact File

Inland Roussillon is not well supplied with hotels and the best place to stay is on the coast near Collioure and Banyuls, except in high summer, when the crowds are excessive.

Information

Comité Départemental du Tourisme des Pyrénées-Roussillon
7 quai de Lattre de Tassigny, 66005 Perpignan. Tel 04 68 34 29 94; fax 04 68 34 71 01.

Office de Tourisme
Avenue de la République, Banyuls. Tel 04 68 88 31 58; fax 04 68 88 36 84.

Office de Tourisme
Place du 18 Juin, 66190 Collioure. Tel 04 68 82 15 47; fax 04 68 82 46 29.

Côtes du Roussillon
19 avenue de Grande Bretagne, 66000 Perpignan. Tel 04 68 51 31 81.
Wine information.

Markets

Céret – Saturday morning
Perpignan (Place de la République) – daily; plus others elsewhere in the city

Festivals and Events

A *Fête des Vendanges* is held in Banyuls in late October.

Where to Buy Wine

There are several well-stocked wine shops in the region.
Comptoir des Crus
1 rue du Marché de Gros, 66000 Perpignan. Tel 04 68 35 54 44; fax 04 68 35 56 11.

Caves du Roussillon
14 avenue Marcelin Albert, 66000 Perpignan. Tel 04 68 54 55 71; fax 04 68 54 53 42.

Caves du Roussillon
19 rue Jules Pams, 66660 Port-Vendres. Tel 04 68 82 42 54; fax 04 68 54 53 42.

Maison de la Vigne et du Vin
Place du 18 juin, 66190 Collioure. Tel 04 68 82 49 00; fax 04 68 82 14 28.

Where to Stay and Eat

Al Fanal (R)
Avenue du Fontaulé, le Port, 66650 Banyuls. Tel 04 68 88 00 81; fax 04 68 88 13 37. (F)
Good Catalan cooking, a touch over-ambitious, and views over the port. Excellent local wines.

Casa Pairal (H)
Impasse des Palmiers, 66190 Collioure. Tel 04 68 82 05 81, fax 04 68 82 52 10. (F)(F)
Although near the village centre, the surrounding park keeps this spacious hotel peaceful.

Le Chapon Fin (R)
18 boulevard Jean-Bourrat, 66000 Perpignan. Tel 04 68 35 14 14; fax 04 68 35 48 18. (F)(F)
Perpignan's top restaurant, offering a blend of *haute cuisine* and staple Catalan dishes.

Château de Jau (le Grill) (R)
66600 Cases-de-Pène. Tel 04 68 38 91 38; fax 04 68 32 91 33. (F)(F)
Outdoor restaurant open only in summer. Delicious grilled food and wines from the estate.

Hôtel les Elmes (H)
Plage des Elmes, 66650 Banyuls. Tel 04 68 88 03 12; fax 04 68 88 53 03. (F)
Starkly modern rooms, as well as some that are more traditionally furnished. Ask for a room with a balcony overlooking the sea. (See la Littorine right.)

Les Feuillants (R)
1 boulevard de La Fayette, 66400 Céret. Tel 04 68 87 37 88; fax 04 68 87 44 68. (F)(F)(F)
Exceptionally stylish restaurant with outstanding food and wine, run by Roussillon's top chef, Didier Banyols, and his wife, a celebrated *sommelier*.

Auberge du Grand Rocher (R)
66720 Caramany. Tel 04 68 84 51 58. (F)

Welcoming restaurant in a remote village, serving simple, well-prepared dishes and good local wines.

Les Graves (H)
9 boulevard Jean Jaurès, 66310 Estagel. Tel 04 68 29 00 84; fax 04 68 29 47 04. (F)
Simple, brightly furnished rooms.

La Littorine (R)
Plage des Elmes, 66650 Banyuls. Tel 04 68 88 03 12; fax 04 68 88 53 03. (F)(F)
The stylish restaurant of the Hotel les Elmes and the place to come for Mediterranean fish and fresh anchovies with red peppers, the local speciality. There are good local wines.

Mas Trilles (H)
Pont de Reynes, 66400 Céret. Tel 04 68 87 38 37. (F)(F)(F)
Luxurious retreat near the charming town of Céret.

Park Hotel (H)
18 boulevard Jean-Bourrat, 66000 Perpignan. Tel 04 68 35 14 14; fax 04 68 35 48 18. (F)(F)
Cosy comfortable rooms, though some can be gloomy.

La Passerelle (R)
1 cours Palmarole, 66000 Perpignan. Tel 04 68 51 30 65. (F)
One of Perpignan's most comfortable restaurants. Try the *supions*, a small squid from the Mediterranean.

Les Templiers (H)(R)
Quai de l'Amirauté, 66190 Collioure. Tel 04 68 98 31 10; fax 04 68 98 01 24. (F)(F)
Friendly, family-run hotel with a famous bar, unchanged for years. Views of the port and castle, but the front rooms can be noisy. Stick to local dishes in the restaurant.

Le Vauban (R)
29 quai Verban, 66000 Perpignan. Tel 04 68 51 05 10; fax 04 68 34 70 61. (F)
A stylish brasserie offering a good choice for a quick meal and a glass of wine.

Wines and Wine Villages

The Côtes du Roussillon wines are mainly red and robust but the regional glory is the fortified wine or Vin Doux Naturel, made mostly from Grenache. The traditional style is wood-aged, rather like an old tawny port, but vintage styles, bottled young, are becoming fashionable.

Banyuls VDN This is Roussillon's most famous fortified wine. It comes from 4 coastal villages, including Collioure and Banyuls itself, and is made mainly from Grenache. The poor soils give low yields that contribute to the wine's power and concentration. Traditional Banyuls is aged in large oak casks, and some wines are 20 or even 30 years old. They have complex aromas of dried fruits, coffee and figs. Rimage wines, which, like vintage port, are bottled young to conserve the fruit flavours, are increasingly fashionable. Banyuls Grand Cru must be at least 75 per cent Grenache Noir and be aged for at least 2½ years in casks.
Best producers: L'ÉTOILE, *du Mas Blanc*, DE LA RECTORIE, TEMPLIERS, *Vial-Magnères*.

Collioure AC This coastal AC overlaps with Banyuls but is restricted to dry red and rosé wines. Grenache is the dominant grape variety, but Mourvèdre, Carignan and Cinsaut are also planted. The wine must be aged for 9 months or more in oak before being bottled. For many visitors, the primary attraction here is the fresh anchovies, rather than the wine: both are delicious. Try the anchovies with red peppers and a chilled Collioure rosé. Then visit the 13th-century Ch. Royal near the harbour.
Best producers: *Clos de Paulilles*, *du Mas Blanc*, DE LA RECTORIE, LA TOUR VIEILLE.

Côtes du Roussillon AC/ Côtes du Roussillon-Villages AC Côtes du Roussillon is a large 4000ha zone, producing mostly red wines. Carignan is the main grape, but its use is now diminishing in favour of superior Grenache, Syrah and Mourvèdre. Cinsaut is less frequently encountered. The white grapes include Maccabéo, Malvoisie, Roussanne, Marsanne and Rolle.

The best vineyard sites for red wine are dispersed among 2000ha north and north-west of Perpignan and these are entitled to the Villages appellation. The grape blend is the same as for Côtes du Roussillon but the vineyard yield is lower. Some producers bottle only their top wines as Villages, using the Côtes du Roussillon label for their lesser wines.

There are some attractive wine villages worth visiting in Roussillon, such as Tautavel, with its museum of prehistory, and the dramatically situated Caramany in the west of the region. South of the main wine zone is Céret, which is charming and has a fine modern art museum, just a few paces away from Roussillon's top restaurant, les Feuillants.
Best producers: BAIXAS, *Casenove*, CAZES, *Força-Réal*, GAUBY, DE JAU, *Mas Crémat*, *Piquemal*, SARDA-MALET, *des Schistes*.

Maury VDN A Grand Cru of Rivesaltes in a remote region flanking the Agly river. The schist vineyards, planted 90 per cent with Grenache Noir, are arid and low-yielding, giving rich fortified wines that are plummier than those of Banyuls. Some of these wines are now being produced in a Vintage style. Traditional Maury is partly aged in glass jars called *bonbonnes*. They are left outdoors in all weathers to induce a measure of oxidation, which gives a sherry-like taste known as *rancio*; this style is also found in Banyuls.
Best producers: MAS AMIEL, *Maury co-operative*, *la Pléiade*.

Muscat de Rivesaltes VDN These are fortified wines, made from either Muscat à Petits Grains or Muscat of Alexandria (or a blend of the two). They are produced throughout the Rivesaltes area and also in Banyuls and are bottled and sold very young to preserve the inimitable perfumed, grapy fruit of Muscat.
Best producers: *see Rivesaltes*.

Rivesaltes VDN This vast AC overlaps with Côtes du Roussillon and other ACs in the region. It covers a variety of styles of fortified wine. There are Ambré wines, golden-coloured from Grenache Blanc or Gris, and dark copper Tuillé wines from Grenache Noir.
Best producers: BAIXAS, *Casenove*, CAZES, *Piquemal*, SARDA-MALET.

Young wine is left to mature outside for several years at the Cellier des Templiers, Banyuls' large co-operative.

In the Pyrenean foothills the Pic du Canigou, snow-capped for much of the year, towers over the Côtes du Roussillon vineyards west of Perpignan. Here at Vinca in the arid Têt Valley the countryside is harsh and barren and grapes are the only viable crop. Roussillon's red wines are mainly made from Carignan but other, superior varieties such as Cinsaut, Grenache and Mourvèdre are being used now in greater quantities. The free-standing vines are trained using the traditional *gobelet* system, which is best suited to low-yielding vines and which produces a compact, wind-resistant bush.

A-Z of Main Wine Producers

Twenty years ago in the south of France, you would have found a sea of vines, most of which belonged to small proprietors who sent their crop to co-operatives more interested in quantity than quality. When it became apparent that there was no future in producing mediocre bulk wines, there was a swift reappraisal: co-operatives invested heavily to improve quality and pressured their growers to lower yields, while individual growers with a passion for wine left the co-operatives and set up their own estates. There have always been outstanding estates in ACs such as Bandol and Châteauneuf-du-Pape, but now the quest for quality has spread across the whole region with amazing rapidity. The following is a selection of top estates, with wine quality the main criterion for inclusion.

Key to Symbols
Visiting arrangements ⊘ Visitors welcome ⊘ By appointment
⊗ No visitors.
Wine styles made ⦿ Red wine ⦾ White wine ⦿ Rosé wine
Vin doux naturel Sweet wines.
Page numbers refer to the tour featuring the producer.

Gilbert Alquier et Fils
34600 Faugères. Tel 04 67 23 07 89; fax 04 67 95 30 51. ⊘⦿⦾
pp.49, 54
Since Gilbert Alquier's death in 1990 this estate has been run by his two sons. The top wines, Maison Jaune, which is half Syrah, and les Bastides, which is mostly Syrah, are aged in oak for at least 14 months. These wines, of great depth and complexity, deserve to be better known.

Domaine de l'Amandine
Quartier Bel Air, 84110 Séguret. Tel 04 90 46 12 39; fax 04 90 46 16 64. ⊘⦿⦾ pp.14, 19
Despite its use of barriques, this is a resolutely old-fashioned estate. The Séguret is made from grapes that are only partially destemmed, giving an extra tannic dimension to the wines. The blend is half Grenache, half Syrah, and the wines are aged in older wood for at least 2 years. The red wines are gutsy and packed with flavour but the whites are less successful.

Domaine d'Aupilhac
28 rue du Plo, 34150 Montpeyroux. Tel 04 67 96 61 19; fax 04 67 96 67 24. ⊘⦿⦾
pp.48, 54, 55
Sylvain Fadat has achieved a formidable reputation for powerful, well-structured red wines. Vinification is traditional, aiming at thorough extraction to give wines for cellaring. His Coteaux du Languedoc is made from equal parts of Carignan, Syrah, Mourvèdre and Grenache, and is bottled without fining or filtration. He also makes a pure Carignan from very old vines. His barrel-fermented white wine is hefty, with impressive fruit.

Cave des Vignerons de Baixas
14 avenue Joffre, 66390 Baixas. Tel 04 68 64 22 37; fax 04 68 64 26 70. ⊘⦿⦾⦿ pp.64, 69
An enormous co-operative, vinifying grapes from 2100ha, but quality is high. The Côtes du Roussillon wines are soundly made, but the Villages ones are superior, especially Cuvée des Terres Rouge, in unoaked and oaked versions. The top wines – oaked Villages, fine Muscat de Rivesaltes and vintage Rivesaltes – are labelled Château les Pins.

Domaines les Bastides
Route de St-Canadet, 13610 le Puy-Ste-Réparade. Tel 04 42 61 97 66; fax 04 61 84 45. ⊘⦿⦾⦿ pp.37, 39

Despite high, north-facing vineyards, Jean Salen routinely harvests Cabernet and Grenache with high potential alcohol. There are two red wines. The regular Cuvée is mostly Grenache, but the superlative Cuvée Spéciale is half Cabernet. Both wines, aged in large oak casks rather than barriques, are exceptional value.

Château de Beaucastel
84350 Courthézon. Tel 04 90 70 70 60; fax 04 90 70 25 24. ⊘⦿
⦾ pp.20, 25, 27
This large organic estate is one of the few to use all 13 Châteauneuf grape varieties, but it is the high proportion of Mourvèdre that gives Beaucastel its character. The whites are also outstanding, especially the expensive Roussanne Vieilles Vignes. Prices have risen considerably in recent years, but the Côtes du Rhône Coudoulet offers a similar experience at lesser cost.

Château de Belle-Coste
30132 Caissargues. Tel 04 66 20 26 48; fax 04 66 20 16 90. ⊘⦿
⦾⦿ pp.30, 31
The estate's top wines are labelled Cuvée St-Marc. Bernard de Tremblay has grown 'experimental' Viognier for the past 11 years, and his delicious white St-Marc is the only Costières de Nîmes wine made overwhelmingly from Viognier.

Domaines Bunan
83740 la Cadière d'Azur. Tel 04 94 98 72 76; fax 04 94 98 60 05. ⊘⦿⦾⦿ pp.41, 43
This large estate offers wines under three labels. Moulin des Costes and Mas de la Rouvière are the standard range. The Ch. de la Rouvière, made only in top vintages, is Mourvèdre from low-yielding vines and needs bottle age. Bunan also makes a

delicious, inexpensive Vin de Pays de Mont Caume from Cabernet Sauvignon.

Domaine de Cabasse
84110 Séguret. Tel 04 90 46 91 12; fax 04 90 46 94 01. ✔️❗️⏱️ ❗️ pp.15, 19
The Swiss Alfred Haeni makes a range of sophisticated modern wines, with some barrique-aging for the top wine, Casa Bassa. The white Côtes du Rhône is spicy but lacks complexity; the rosé is robust yet fresh. There is a superb, high-priced Gigondas.

Cave de Cairanne
Route de Ste-Cécile, 84290 Cairanne. Tel: 04 90 30 82 05; fax 04 90 30 74 03. ✔️❗️⏱️❗️ pp.13, 18
The best wines from this well-run co-operative reflect a careful choice of grapes and traditional vinification. The red Réserve des Voconces, from old vines, and the Cuvée Antique, with a dash of aging in new oak, are excellent value. White Carte Passion is barrel-fermented, but the unoaked white is far livelier.

Château Calissanne
13680 Lançon-de-Provence. Tel 04 90 42 63 03; fax 04 90 42 40 00. ✔️❗️⏱️❗️ pp.37, 39
The vineyards here produce 2 of Provence's most opulent red wines: Cuvée Prestige and Clos Victoire. The Prestige, a blend of Cabernet, Syrah and Mourvèdre, is a rich, silky wine that needs bottle age to show at its best. The lack of Mourvèdre in Clos Victoire makes it slightly more approachable. Both wines are aged in barriques, as is the white Clos Victoire, from Clairette and Sauvignon. The wines are pricy.

Château de Capitoul
Route de Gruissan, 11100 Narbonne. Tel 04 68 49 23 30; fax 04 68 49 55 71. ✔️❗️⏱️❗️ pp.61, 63
The largest estate in la Clape has much improved in recent years. Rosé features strongly, and is made principally from Grenache. Of the two reds, Grand Terroir is almost all Syrah. The white Grand Terroir is made from Marsanne, Roussanne and Rolle in equal quantities, with fermentation in new barriques. Viognier, similarly vinified, emerges as rich and powerful (and expensive).

Cave Coopérative Castelmaure
11360 Embres-et-Castelmaure. Tel 04 68 45 91 83; fax 04 68 45 93 56. ✔️❗️⏱️❗️ pp.60, 63
Despite its ramshackle appearance, this small co-operative is technically progressive. The growers make great efforts to keep vineyard yields low, and the top wines, such as Pompadour which is dominated by old Carignan, are decidedly concentrated. The best white is Dame d'Embres, a barrique-fermented Grenache Blanc.

Domaine Cazes
4 rue F. Ferrer, 66600 Rivesaltes. Tel 04 68 64 08 26; fax 04 68 64 69 79. ✔️❗️⏱️❗️ pp.64, 69
This long-established estate produces outstanding wines. The basic ranges, such as Cuvée du Chalet and Canon du Maréchal, are sound, but pale beside the Côtes du Roussillon and the impressive Villages red. The otherwise traditional Cazes brothers are impressed by the quality of Bordeaux varieties in their vineyards and since 1993

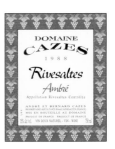

have made le Crédo, an oak-aged Bordeaux blend with real panache. The Rivesaltes are very fine.

Domaine le Clos des Cazaux
84190 Vacqueyras. Tel 04 90 65 85 83; fax 04 90 65 83 94. ✔️❗️ ⏱️ pp.15, 18, 19
The vineyards are divided between Gigondas and Vacqueyras, with 3 different Vacqueyras wines: Cuvée Réserve should be drunk young for its appealing fruit; Cuvée St-Roch is from old Grenache and Syrah vines; and Cuvée des Templiers is dominated by Syrah. The white is one of the few good Vacqueyras examples; the Gigondas is first-rate.

Clos des Centeilles
34210 Siran. Tel 04 68 91 52 18; fax 04 68 91 65 92. ✔️❗️ pp.51, 55
Despite the dilapidated winery, the Clos produces the most characterful of all Minervois wines. Soils are exceptional and only very ripe grapes are used, so the wines are powerfully flavoured. Clos Centeilles is made from old vines and aged for 2 years in barriques, but there is also a pure Carignan, called Carignanissime, and a pure Cinsaut, Cuvée Capitelle. Pinot Noir also features, labelled Guigniers de Centeilles.

VISITING WINE PRODUCERS

Unlike, say, the châteaux of Bordeaux, the estates of southern France pride themselves on extending a warm welcome. **Appointments** are rarely required in summer, but out of season it is sensible to telephone ahead to check whether anyone will be available to receive you. **English-speaking staff** are to be found at some co-operatives. At the smaller estates the owner or wine-maker is more likely to show you around; he/she will be more knowledgeable about the domaine, but possibly less fluent in English. **Lunchtime** in rural France is still an important occasion, so ensure that you don't arrive at a property between 12 and 2pm. **Harvest time** (early September/mid-October) is a busy time of the year and people may not always have time to stop to help you. Visits are not recommended unless the domaine employs a full-time guide.

Tastings will probably consist of samples of the most recently bottled vintage(s). Most domaines have a tasting room in which the proprietor pours wines for visitors. You are not obliged to buy, but if you spend a good deal of time talking to the owner and like the wines, it won't go amiss to buy a bottle or two. **Spitoons**, or *crachoirs*, are usually provided and it is best to use them in order to keep a clean palate. **Credit cards** are accepted by most estates.

Clos du Mont Olivet

15 avenue St-Joseph, 84230
Châteauneuf-du-Pape. Tel 04 90
83 72 46; fax 04 90 83 51 75. ✓
⊕ⓌⓉ pp.25, 27
Nothing ever seems to change at
this wonderfully traditional
estate. The vines are very old,
and Grenache always dominates
the rich, heady red. The grapes
are not destemmed, so Mont
Olivet can be tough in its youth.
The white is less interesting.

Domaine Clos des Papes

13 avenue Pierre de Luxembourg,
84230 Châteauneuf-du-Pape.
Tel 04 90 83 70 13; fax 04 90 83
50 87. ✓ⓌⓉ pp.24, 27
Viticulture and vinification are
meticulous. The red is a blend of
Grenache and Mourvèdre and
ages well. The exemplary white
can also be drunk young but
improves after 7 years in bottle.

Commanderie de Peyrassol

83340 Flassans-sur-Issole. Tel 04
94 69 71 02; fax 04 94 59 69 23.
✓ⓌⓉⓌ p.35, 39
Françoise Rigord produces a
broad range of wines, including
3 different rosés. The overall
quality is good, but the wines are
expensive, especially the top
Cabernet-dominated Marie-
Estelle, which is aged in new
oak. Sweet wines are a speciality
but lack the body of a true Vin
Doux Naturel.

Cellier Charles Cros

11200 Fabrezan. Tel 04 68 43 61
18; fax 04 68 43 51 88. ✓Ⓦ
Ⓦ pp.59, 63
With the emphasis on Syrah
rather than Carignan, this
excellent co-operative makes
good, inexpensive modern-style
Corbières at all levels. Both
white and red Arpège, the basic
wines, are satisfying everyday
drinking. More characterful are
Prieuré de la Bernède,
Symphonie and Delicatesse.

Château des Estanilles

Lenthéric, 34480 Cabrerolles.
Tel 04 67 90 29 25; fax 04 67 90
10 99. ✓ⓌⓉⓌ pp.49, 54
Michel Louison named his best
vineyard Clos du Fou because
only a lunatic would have gone

to the trouble of reclaiming this
rocky site. His tenacity has paid
off, and Estanilles is celebrated
for its range of densely fruity
wines. Louison's basic Faugères,
Vin Tradition, is sound, but the
excitement begins with his
Syrah-dominated Prestige wine.
He takes rosé seriously too,
fermenting Mourvédre in oak.
The white is mostly Marsanne
and is partially barrel-fermented.

L'Étoile

66650 Banyuls. Tel 04 68 88 00
10; fax 04 68 88 15 10. ✓ⓌⓌ
pp.67, 69
This medium-sized co-operative
produces good Banyuls in styles
ranging from off-dry white to
long-aged traditional to fruity
Vintage. The best wines – Paillé
Hors d'Age, Sélect Vieux and
Grande Réserve – are traditional.

Domaine de la Ferme Blanche

13260 Cassis. Tel 04 42 01 00 74;
fax 04 42 01 73 94. ✓ⓌⓉⓌ
pp.40, 43
Unusually, la Ferme Blanche
produces 2 different white wines.
The regular wine contains 4 or 5
different grape varieties, but the
Blanc de Blancs is a foretaste of
Cassis to come, since it contains
only Clairette and Marsanne,
which in future will be required
to dominate Cassis white wines.
Reds have some barrique-aging.

Château Fortia

84230 Châteauneuf-du-Pape.
Tel 04 90 83 70 06; fax 04 90 83
51 03. ✓ⓌⓉ pp.23, 27
The red wine is highly
traditional, with a high proportion
of Grenache; the white is also a
typical Châteauneuf blend. After
a dull patch in the early 1980s,
when the wines were rather light,
the estate is back on form with
full-bodied wines in a fairly
austere style.

Domaine le Galantin

83330 le Plan-du-Castellet.
Tel 04 94 98 75 94; fax 04 94 90
29 55. ✓ⓌⓉⓌ pp.42, 43
A modest family estate which has
long been an excellent source for
traditional Bandol at fair prices.
The red is 80 per cent
Mourvèdre and Achille Pascal
does not start harvesting until the
grapes have high potential
alcohol. Before 1994 the grapes
were not destemmed, so some
vintages could be a bit tough. But
Galantin excels in very ripe years.

Domaine Gauby

Le Faradjal, 66600 Calce. Tel 04
68 64 35 19; fax 04 68 64 41 77.
✓ⓌⓉⓌ pp.65, 69
This outstanding estate produces
a large range of wines. Yields are
very low, giving wines of
enormous concentration – and
high prices. The red Villages is
excellent; look out, too, for oaky
varietal wines, notably Viognier
and les Centenaires made from
Grenache Blanc.

Domaines Gavoty

Le Grand Campdumy, 83440
Cabasse. Tel 04 94 69 72 39;
fax 04 94 59 64 04. ✓ⓌⓉⓌ
pp.36, 39
Today Bernard Gavoty's niece
makes the wine here, the best of
which are labelled Clarendon.
The white is made from Rolle
and is not usually oak-aged. The
rosé has enough weight to
accompany strongly flavoured
foods. The reds, from Syrah,
Grenache and Cabernet, benefit
from a few years of bottle age.

Domaine les Goubert

84190 Gigondas. Tel 04 90 65
86 38; fax 04 90 65 81 52. ✓Ⓦ
Ⓣ pp.15, 18, 19
Jean-Pierre Cartier was the first
producer to release a Gigondas
aged in a large proportion of
new oak, Cuvée Florence. His
more traditional Gigondas and
Beaumes-de-Venise are superbly
concentrated. His white Sablet is
now also fermented in new oak.

Château Hélène

11800 Barbaira. Tel 04 68 79 00
69; fax 04 68 79 06 97. ✓ⓌⓌ
Ⓦ pp.58, 63

There is a pleasant welcome at this functional winery. The wines all bear classical names and are sound, fairly concentrated Corbières. The basic range is called Pénélope, and the more ambitious wines are Cuvée Ulysse, mainly Syrah and aged for 6 months in older barriques, and Cuvée Hélène de Troie. The red version is mostly Syrah and is aged in new oak; the white is barrel-fermented Grenache Blanc and Roussanne.

Domaine de l'Hortus
34270 Valflaunès. Tel 04 67 55 31 20; fax 04 67 55 38 03. ✓●💧🍷 pp.47, 55
In 1978 Jean Orliac restored the vineyards here, and since 1990 he has been producing acclaimed red wines based on Syrah and Mourvèdre. The Cuvée Classique is aged in older barriques, whereas the more concentrated Grande Cuvée spends 15 months in 50 per cent new oak. The flavourful whites are sold as Vins de Pays.

Domaine de l'Hospitalet
Route de Narbonne Plage, 11100 Narbonne. Tel 04 68 45 34 47; fax 04 68 45 23 49. ✓💧🍷🍷 pp.61, 63
Founded in 1990, the Hospitalet complex in la Clape would not look amiss in California's Napa Valley. There is a very large range of wines, arguably too many. The vast barrique cellar is used to full advantage, and even some rosés are aged in oak. Initial vintages have lacked concentration, possibly because of the youth of the vines.

Château de Jau
66600 Cases-de-Pène. Tel 04 68 38 91 38; fax 04 68 32 91 33. ✓●🍷 pp.65, 69
This large Côtes du Roussillon estate produces a sound red in a soft, plush style. Also available are excellent rosés and reds from Clos de Paulilles in Collioure.

Domaine des Jougla
Prades-sur-Vernazobres, 34360 St-Chinian. Tel 04 67 38 06 02; fax 04 67 38 17 74. ✓●💧 pp.50, 55

Alain Jougla produces 3 red wines from his schist and limestone soils. Cuvée Classique blends the standard St-Chinian varieties and ages the wine in large casks; Cuvée Tradition, made from older vines, is more concentrated; and Cuvée Signée is made only from schist soils and is partly aged in barriques as well as older casks. The wines are consistent, stylish, have good fruit and are good value.

Château de Lastours
11490 Portel. Tel 04 68 48 29 17; fax 04 68 48 29 14. ✓●💧 pp.60, 63
This enormous Corbières estate, with more than 100ha of vines set in a bowl of hills, produces excellent wine. The despised Carignan grape features strongly, but the fruit quality is very good. Choose between the unoaked Cuvée Simone Descamps and the Fûts de Chêne, which spends a year in small barrels. The white wine can be rich and heady.

Cave Coopérative de Laurens
34480 Laurens. Tel 04 67 90 28 23; fax 04 67 90 25 47. ✓●💧 🍷 pp.49, 54
About one-third of all Faugères is made here, so the basic style is fairly commercial, relying heavily on carbonic maceration. Most reds are dominated by Grenache and Carignan. The two best wines are Ch. de Laurens and Valentin Duc, which is made in a softer, more accessible style.

Domaine Maby
30126 Tavel. Tel 04 66 50 03 40; fax 04 66 50 43 12. ✓●💧 🍷 pp.25, 27
A leading producer of Lirac, Maby makes a red that is always a well-structured blend of Grenache and Mourvèdre. It is

not even bottled until almost 3 years after the harvest. The white is good, and there is a Cuvée Prestige fermented in new barriques. The Tavel is reliable and well-flavoured.

Maîtres Vignerons de la Presqu'Île de St-Tropez
Carrefour de la Foux, 83580 Gassin. Tel 04 94 56 32 04; fax 04 94 43 42 57. ✓●💧🍷 pp.34, 39
In 1964, 9 large estates behind St-Tropez joined forces to sell their wines through the Maîtres Vignerons, which also turns their grapes into inexpensive but well-made wines such as Cèpe d'Or and Carte Noire. The best wine is Château de Pampelonne, a lightly oaked red. They also sell produce, and in summer farmers' markets are held in the forecourt.

Château Mansenoble
11700 Moux. Tel 04 68 43 93 39; fax 04 68 43 97 21. ✓●🍷 pp.58, 63
Mansenoble was bought by the Belgian wine writer Guido Jansegers and his wife in 1992. Despite their lack of wine-making experience, they have won great acclaim for their reds, especially the Syrah-dominated Réserve, which is aged for 13 months in barriques. Jansegers ensures that only very ripe grapes are picked.

Mas Amiel
66460 Maury. Tel 04 68 29 01 02; fax 04 68 29 17 82. ✓ pp.66, 69
A large estate with a magnificent raftered winery, where immense oak casks contain fortified wine previously aged outdoors for a year in glass *bonbonnes*. This process gives traditional Maury, but since 1985 Mas Amiel has also been producing wines in a vintage style, bottled young.

Mas de la Dame
13520 Maussane. Tel 04 90 54 32 24; fax 04 90 54 40 67. ✓● 💧🍷 pp.29, 31
This 17th-century les Baux estate produces a range of wines at various prices. The basic red is Cuvée Gourmande, while the Réserve is aged for longer before

bottling. The red Cuvée de la Stèle, from very old vines, is very good value.

Mas de Daumas Gassac
34150 Aniane. Tel 04 67 57 71 28; fax 04 67 57 41 03. ✓🍷☺ pp.44, 47-8, 55
A remarkable estate, created in the 1970s by Aimé Guibert on an outstanding red soil, which gives wines of great power and longevity. A Bordeaux blend, Daumas Gassac is rich in extract and tannin, a big, old-fashioned wine with tremendous depth of flavour. The equally astonishing white is a blend of several varieties, including Viognier and Chardonnay, with highly floral aromas; it should be drunk young.

Mas de Gourgonnier
Le Destet, 13890 Mouriès. Tel 04 90 47 50 45; fax 04 90 47 51 36. ✓🍷☺🍷 pp.30, 31
This splendid estate, run on organic lines, lies in a remote spot of the Alpilles. The reds are rich and spicy, especially the Réserve, which contains equal amounts of Cabernet, Syrah and Grenache. The rosé has ample body but can be a touch earthy. The white has improved greatly in recent years.

Mas Jullien
34725 Jonquières. Tel 04 67 96 60 01; fax 04 67 96 60 50. ✓🍷☺ p.54
It is hard to keep track of Olivier Jullien's wines, for he is always experimenting with new blends. But despite his eccentricities, the wines are much in demand and are rarely on sale at the winery.

Château Mas Neuf
Gallician, 30600 Vauvert. Tel 04 66 73 33 23; fax 04 66 73 33 49. ✓🍷☺🍷 pp.30, 31
Restless and vigorous, Olivier Gibelin constantly experiments with new vinification techniques and products such as Sangria made from Carignan. His whites are particularly enjoyable, and all the wines are sensibly priced.

Château Maurel Fonsalade
34490 Causses et Veyran. Tel 04 67 89 57 90; fax 04 67 89 73 04. ✓🍷☺🍷 pp.49, 55

Maurel Fonsalade is an isolated estate set in beautiful countryside, but there is nothing rustic about the wine-making. Soils are varied, allowing 3 different blends of red to be made. The delicious rosé is barrel-fermented and the first whites were made in 1997.

Producteurs du Mont Tauch
11350 Tuchan. Tel 04 68 45 41 08; fax 04 68 45 45 29. ✓🍷☺ 🍷 pp.61, 63
This large co-operative has always had a good reputation for Fitou and accounts for 45 per cent of its production. With a substantial proportion of old Carignan in the blend, the wines are aged for 2 years before release. There are numerous blends and single-domaine wines, such as the delicious Ch. de Ségure. The top blend is Terroir de Tuchan, but the high proportion of Syrah makes it atypical, and some prefer the rich, but more rustic, Prestige de Paziols.

Château Mourgues du Grès
30300 Beaucaire. Tel 04 66 59 46 10; fax 04 66 59 34 21. ✓🍷 🍷 pp.30, 31
François Collard is a young grower who aims for quality. His wines may not be the cheapest in the region, but they are among the best. The reds are Syrah-dominated, and Collard's top cuvée, Terre d'Argence, is made from old vines. These are wines with remarkable purity of fruit enhanced by supple tannins. The rosé is outstanding, too.

Château la Nerthe
Route de Sorgues, 84230 Châteauneuf-du-Pape. Tel 04 90 83 70 11; fax 04 90 83 79 69. ✓🍷☺ pp.24, 27
This large, well-equipped estate produces sophisticated wines, including red Cuvée de Cadettes and white Clos de Beauvenir

which are aged in partially new oak. Two-thirds of the regular red is aged in older barriques. These oaky wines have a strong following despite their high prices. The regular red Cuvée has finesse rather than power.

Domaine de l'Oratoire St-Martin
Route de St-Romain, 84290 Cairanne. Tel 04 90 30 82 07; fax 04 90 30 74 27. ✓🍷☺ pp.13, 18
The vines here at this Côtes du Rhône-Villages estate are, on average, 50 years old – and it shows in the wines, which are deeply flavoured and have considerable capacity for aging. The best wines are Prestige, with 40 per cent Mourvèdre and very old Grenache, and Haut-Coustias, mostly Mourvèdre and Syrah and aged in barriques. The delicious white Haut-Coustias is pure Marsanne.

Cave de l'Ormarine
1 avenue du Picpoul, 34850 Pinet. Tel 04 67 77 03 10; fax 04 67 77 76 23. ✓🍷☺ pp.48, 55
This co-operative is responsible for at least half the sales of Picpoul de Pinet, the crisp white that goes so well with shellfish. The basic wine is Carte Noire, with a fresh lemongrass nose, but the more expensive Duc de Morny has more character.

Domaine les Pallières
84190 Gigondas. Tel 04 90 65 85 07. ✓🍷 pp.15, 18
The Roux family have owned this estate for 250 years, and the present owner, Pierre Roux, remains conservative in his wine-making. The wines are bottled at up to 6 years after the harvest. The result is slightly rustic and leathery, but full of character and long-lived.

Château Pech-Céleyran
11110 Salles d'Aude. Tel 04 68 33 50 04; fax 04 68 33 36 12. ✓🍷☺🍷 pp.61, 63
About half the wines from this large estate are Vins de Pays, the remainder are la Clape, the AC vines occupying the higher vineyards. The reds are aged in

large old casks and occasionally in barriques. The white is mostly Marsanne and Roussanne, since Bourboulenc, the approved la Clape grape, is not very successful here. There is a fine range of varietal wines: unoaked and oaked Chardonnays, Viognier and an unusual Pinot Noir.

Domaine de Piaugier
84110 Sablet. Tel 04 90 46 96 49; fax 04 90 46 99 48. ✅🔵🍷 pp.15, 19
Jean-Marc Autran produces 3 different reds from Sablet, each from a different site. Tenebi is the most unusual, blending Grenache and Cunoise. He also makes an excellent Gigondas, and his barrel-fermented white wines contain a high proportion of Viognier.

Château de Pibarnon
83740 la Cadière d'Azur. Tel 04 94 90 12 73; fax 04 94 90 12 98. ✅🔵🍷 pp.41, 43
Pibarnon is a superlative estate. The owner, Comte Henri de St-Victor, modestly attributes this to the limestone- and fossil-rich soil. The red wine is almost entirely Mourvèdre, yet is supple from the outset, although top vintages benefit greatly from bottle-age. No new oak is used. The delicious white is a mix of different varieties, including Viognier and Petit Manseng.

Château Pradeaux
83270 St-Cyr. Tel 04 94 32 10 21; fax 04 94 32 16 02. ✅🔵🍷 pp.42, 43
This fine estate, owned by the Portalis family since 1752, is highly traditional. The grapes are not destemmed, and the wine is aged up to 5 years in casks before bottling. This allows the high Mourvèdre content to soften up. Pradeaux can be dense and unapproachable when young and not all vintages are successful, but for many wine lovers a mature Pradeaux is among the best of all Bandols.

Prieuré de St-Jean de Bébian
Route de Nizas, 34120 Pézenas. Tel 04 67 98 13 60; fax 04 67 98 22 24. ✅🔵🍷 pp.48, 54

Alain Roux, the former owner of this estate, made wonderful wines. His Grenache came from Ch. Rayas, his Syrah from Chave in Hermitage, his Mourvèdre from Domaine Tempier. The blend gave a hefty dark wine that aged superbly. In 1994 a leading wine journalist, Chantal Lecouty, and her husband bought the estate. Little has changed, but there will be a more careful grape selection and greater use of new oak; white wine production will increase. Prices are high.

Domaine Raspail-Ay
84190 Gigondas. Tel 04 90 65 83 01; fax 04 90 65 89 55. ✅🔵🍷 pp.15, 18
If the test of a good winemaker is an ability to make fine wine in poor vintages, then Dominique Ay qualifies for the description. His Gigondas is always deep-coloured, full-bodied and packed with fruit. He has no interest in barrique-aging, preferring large old casks, and rarely needs to fine or filter. The results are arguably the finest Gigondas.

Château Rayas
84230 Châteauneuf-du-Pape. Tel 04 90 83 73 09. ✅🔵🍷 pp.25, 27
Jacques Reynaud is formidably shy and eccentric, so any attempt to make an appointment will probably be rebuffed. The vines, mainly Grenache, are very old and low-yielding, giving the wine tremendous concentration and at its majestic best it is truly great. It is priced accordingly, and Pignan (a Châteauneuf) and Fonsalette (a stunning Côtes du Rhône) are better value.

Domaine de la Rectorie
65 avenue du Puig del Mas, 66650 Banyuls. Tel 04 68 88 13 45; fax 04 68 88 18 55. ✅🔵🍷 pp.67, 69

The leading Banyuls estate, la Rectorie makes superb, long-lived Collioure as well as Banyuls. The Parcé brothers produce 3 different Collioures, all aged in barriques, although they are sparing with new oak. The Banyuls is mostly made in a Vintage style. There is also a drier Banyuls called Elizabeth, and a flavourful dry, unfortified *rancio* wine called Vin de Pierre.

Château Revelette
13490 Jouques. Tel 04 42 63 75 43; fax 04 42 67 62 04. ✅🔵🍷 pp.36, 39
The German winemaker Peter Fischer acquired this estate in 1985. The vineyards are high up and winters are cold, so all his wines have a bracing acidity and vigour. His best wines are labelled Grand Vin de Revelette. The white is Chardonnay, barrel-fermented but subtle and far removed from a broad, buttery New-World style. The red, half Syrah, half Cabernet, is aged in older barriques for 12 months.

Domaine Richeaume
13114 Puyloubier. Tel 04 42 66 31 27; fax 04 42 66 30 59. ✅🔵🍷 p.39
Henning Hoesch created this fine estate flanking Mont Ste-Victoire in 1972. The estate, run on organic lines, produces an impressive red wine, rich, oaky and well structured. Cuvée Tradition blends Grenache and Cabernet, and there are 2 other wines, one mostly Cabernet, the other mostly Syrah.

Château Romanin
13210 St-Rémy-de-Provence. Tel 04 90 92 45 87; fax 04 90 92 24 36. ✅🔵🍷 pp.30, 31
Romanin is worth visiting as a tourist attraction as much as for its wines. The estate is designed to harmonize with the phases of the moon and other planetary movements. The modern winery, tunnelled into the rock, also reflects biodynamic principles. The wines are good but not yet exciting. Try the oaked white, the delightful rosé and the Vin Cuit, a traditional Provençal sweet wine.

Château la Roque

34270 Fontanès. Tel 04 67 55 34 47; fax 04 67 55 10 18. ✓①① ① pp.47, 55
Jack Boutin is a long-established owner in Pic St-Loup, and his wines are very well made, including the white Clos des Bénédictins and the outstanding red Cupa Numismae, made from low-yielding Mourvèdre and Syrah and aged for 15 months in one-third new oak.

Cave les Vins de Roquebrun

Avenue des Orangers, 34460 Roquebrun. Tel 04 67 89 64 35; fax 04 67 89 5793. ✓①①① pp.50, 55
This co-operative produces wines considerably superior to those of many St-Chinian estates. There are 2 basic styles of red: Syrah-dominated Roches Noires and Mourvèdre-dominated Prestige. Identical wines aged in barriques are sold as Ch. Roquebrun and Sir de Roc Brun respectively.

Château St-Auriol

11220 Lagrasse. Tel 04 68 43 15 10; fax 04 68 43 15 32. ✓①① p.63
Jean-Paul Salvagnac and Claude Vialade make delicious, elegant reds, and the white, from Bourboulenc, Marsanne, Roussanne and Grenache Blanc and barrel-fermented in new oak, is among Corbières' best.

Château Ste-Roseline

83460 les Arcs. Tel 04 94 73 32 57; fax 04 94 47 53 06. ✓①① ① pp.35, 39
Bernard Teillaud acquired this splendid estate in 1994 and aims to transform it into a cultural centre. The 2 ranges of red, rosé and white − Tête de Cuvée is the better one − spend some time in barriques and the style has not changed under the new owner. The wines are good but pricy.

Domaine Santa-Duc

84190 Gigondas. Tel 04 90 65 84 49; fax 04 90 54 81 63. ✓① pp.15, 18
Yves Gras, the rising star of the Gigondas AC, insists on low yields and late harvesting to

ensure the finest quality grapes which are mostly Grenache Noir and Mourvèdre.

Domaine Sarda-Malet

12 chemin de Ste-Barbe, 66000 Perpignan. Tel 04 68 56 72 38; fax 04 68 56 47 60. ✓①① pp.66, 69
This fine estate makes little use of carbonic maceration. The reds are fruity and robust, especially the Étiquette Noire and the Terroir Mailloles. The white Côtes is vigorous and has good acidity, and there is a delicious late-harvest Malvoisie called l'Abandon, as well as splendid 20-year-old Rivesaltes.

Château Simone

13590 Meyreuil. Tel 04 42 66 92 58. ✓①①① pp.37, 39
The leading estate in Palette, one of the tiniest ACs in France, is the elegant Ch. Simone. The grapes here benefit from a special mesoclimate and some vines are 100 years old; the wine-making is traditional. The white, made mostly from Clairette in a gently oxidative style, is highly esteemed and ages well, as does the robust red. But because of its rarity, the wine has become overpriced.

Domaine de la Soumade

84110 Rasteau. Tel 04 90 46 11 26. ✓① pp.13, 19
The impassioned André Roméro runs this estate, where the wines are vinified to enable them to age well. The top wines are Cuvée Prestige and Cuvée Confiance, which is produced only in outstanding vintages. There is also a delicious Rasteau Doux.

Domaine Tempier

83330 le Plan-du-Castellet. Tel 04 94 98 70 21; fax 04 94 90 21 65. ✓①①① pp.41, 42, 43
This estate is now run by Lucien Peyraud's children and grandchildren. There are no fewer than 5 red wines in the range. The basic wine is Cuvée Classique, while Cuvée Spéciale benefits from a higher proportion of Mourvèdre in the blend. Of the 3 single-vineyard wines, Migoua, Tourtine and Cabassaou, only the last is made

from 100 per cent Mourvèdre. Migoua is the most elegant. The wines are reasonably priced.

Cellier des Templiers

Route du Mas Reig, 66650 Banyuls. Tel 04 68 98 36 70; fax 04 68 88 00 84. ✓① pp.67, 69
This enormous co-operative sells 67 per cent of all Banyuls and 85 per cent of all Collioure wines. So it is not surprising that the co-operative produces at least 4 red Collioures, as well as several Banyuls. The traditional Banyuls are better than the Rimage, and there are superb, but expensive, old Cuvées, such as Viviane le Roy and the more peppery, less sweet Henri Vidal.

Domaines des Terres Blanches

13210 St-Rémy-de-Provence. Tel 04 90 95 91 66; fax 04 90 95 99 04. ✓①①① pp.30, 31
Like many les Baux estates, this is run on organic lines. The wines are very good and the range varies each vintage. There are sporadic special Cuvées made, in seeming defiance of AC rules, from pure Syrah, Cabernet, Sauvignon Blanc or Mourvèdre. These wines have high tannin levels and benefit from aging.

Domaine la Tour Boisée

11800 Laure-Minervois. Tel 04 68 78 10 04; fax 04 68 78 10 98. ✓①①① pp.51, 55
This is one of the leading Minervois estates. From perfectly ripe grapes, Jean-Louis Poudou makes wines full of fruit and almost jammy, thanks to high fermentation temperatures. But they also age well, especially the Cuvée Marie-Claude. There are 2 whites − the oaked Cuvée is exceptionally rich − and botrytis wines of scintillating quality.

Domaine de la Tour du Bon

83330 le Brulat-de-Castellet. Tel 04 94 32 61 62; fax 04 94 32

71 69. ⊘⓵⓸⓹ pp.42, 43

Agnès Henry-Hocquard manages this small family estate in Bandol and employs the young and enthusiastic Antoine Pouponneau as her winemaker. Yields are low and the wines are bottled without fining or filtration. The regular wine has delicious fruit, but the star is the Cuvée St-Ferréol, which is pure Mourvèdre partially aged in new oak. The oak-aging here is well judged and rarely obtrusive.

Domaine la Tour Vieille
3 avenue du Mirador, 66190 Collioure. Tel 04 68 82 42 20; fax 04 68 92 38 42. ⊘⓵
pp.66, 69
Although only 12ha in extent, this small estate produces many wines. There are 2 well-extracted red Collioures, of which the finer is usually Puig Oriol. The Vintage Banyuls is sound and Cuvée Francis Contié is aged in glass *bonbonnes* and larger casks. Two specialities are 40-year-old unfiltered Banyuls, labelled Vin de Méditation, and a strong dry *rancio* wine called Cap de Creus.

Domaine de Trévallon
St-Étienne-du-Grès, 13150 Tarascon. Tel 04 90 49 06 00. ⊘⓵⓹ pp.30, 31
In 1974 Eloi Dürrbach planted Cabernet Sauvignon and Syrah on very stony soils flanking the Alpilles. With low yields Dürrbach practised slow fermentation and long aging in large casks with no filtration. The results are rich, delicious, long-lived wines with impeccable balance and elegance. In great demand, the wines are expensive, especially the rare white, a barrel-fermented Roussanne. The authorities condemn the presence of Cabernet here, so les Baux's top wine is now sold as Vin de Pays du Bouches-du-Rhône.

Domaine de Triennes
N560, 83860 Nans-les-Pins. Tel 04 94 78 91 46; fax 04 94 78 65 04. ⊘⓵⓸⓹ pp.36, 39
In 1990, owners of 2 celebrated Burgundy estates – Aubert de Villaine of la Romanée-Conti

and Jacques Seysses of Domaine Dujac – acquired these sheltered vineyards in the Coteaux Varois AC. The current range includes single-varietal bottlings of Viognier, Chardonnay, Merlot and Syrah, and an excellent unfiltered, half Syrah, half Cabernet blend called les Auréliens. As the vines mature these modestly priced wines are improving steadily.

Château de Trinquevedel
30126 Tavel. Tel 04 66 50 04 04; fax 04 66 50 31 66. ⊘⓹
pp.25, 27
The Demoulin family have been producing the wine here since 1936 and their Tavel is a benchmark for the AC. Most of the vines are more than 45 years old and the wine has good concentration. Malolactic fermentation is rare, so the rosé keeps its freshness. After 2 years in bottle it develops more aromatic complexity, but at the expense of its initial fruitiness.

Le Vieux Donjon
9 avenue St-Joseph, 84230 Châteauneuf-du-Pape. Tel 04 90 83 70 03; fax 04 90 83 50 38. ⊘⓵⓹ pp.25, 27
This small estate makes exemplary traditional Châteauneuf-du-Pape. The red is mainly Grenache, the grapes are not destemmed and the wines are bottled after 2 years in cask without fining or filtration. The white wine is delightfully aromatic in its youth.

Vieux Télégraphe
3 route de Châteauneuf-du-Pape, 84370 Bédarrides. Tel 04 90 33 00 31; fax 04 90 33 18 47. ⊘⓵⓹ pp.24, 27
Succulent fruit is the hallmark of this wine, which is vinified in a modern winery and bottled without filtration. Sometimes Vieux Télégraphe lacks the depth and richness of some other

Châteauneuf reds, but it is always balanced and enjoyable. The white is one of the most serious and long-lived in the AC.

Château Vignelaure
83560 Rians. Tel 04 94 80 31 93; fax 04 94 80 53 39. ⊘⓵
pp.36, 39
This substantial estate pioneered Cabernet Sauvignon in the Coteaux d'Aix AC, and its wines were always savoury, structured and long-lived. It is now owned by Hugh Ryman and David O'Brien, and the wines are becoming softer and richer, while still retaining a high proportion of Cabernet.

Château Villerambert-Julien
11160 Caunes-Minervois. Tel 04 68 78 00; fax 04 68 78 05 34. ⊘⓵⓹ pp.51, 55
The château, tasting room, and packaging here are reminiscent of Bordeaux and the wines have a Bordelais elegance. There are 2 red wines: Opéra, a well-balanced, elegant wine, and the more serious Trianon, with 14 months' aging in barriques, and more spice and aging potential. The rosé is lively and delicious.

Domaine de la Vivonne
83330 le Castellet. Tel 04 94 98 70 09; fax 04 94 90 59 98. ⊘⓵⓹ pp.42, 43
Walter Gilpin makes wines of exceptional purity and richness from only Mourvèdre. These Bandols are dark and dense and need at least 5 years in bottle for the marvellous black-fruit flavours to re-emerge. The rosé, which is half Mourvèdre, is best drunk with food.

Château la Voulte-Gasparets
11200 Boutenac. Tel 04 68 27 07 86; fax 04 68 27 41 33. ⊘⓵⓹ pp.60, 63
This is a reliable source of excellent Corbières. Patrick Reverdy uses carbonic maceration for all his reds. The top wine is Cuvée Romain Pauc, using grapes from the best and oldest vineyards. Although both reds spend some time in barriques, very little new oak is used. The white is mainly Grenache Blanc.

Index of Other Wine Producers

For Main Wine Producers see pages 72–79.

Picture Credits
Principal photographer Mick Rock (Cephas Picture Library); other Cephas photographers Hervé Champollion 60; Andy Christodolo 48, 51; Alain Proust 25. Other photographs supplied by Michael Busselle 16, 46, 52, 55, 64, 67; Hughes-Gilbey Picture Library 10.
Publisher's Acknowledgments Trevor Lawrence (map illustrations), Aziz Khan (grape artworks), Steven Marwood (bottle photography).